The Little Schemer

The Little Schemer

Fourth Edition

Daniel P. Friedman

Indiana University
Bloomington, Indiana

Matthias Felleisen

Rice University
Houston, Texas

Drawings by Duane Bibby

Foreword by Gerald J. Sussman

The MIT Press
Cambridge, Massachusetts
London, England

Original edition published as *The Little LISPer*. © 1986, 1974 by Scientific Research Associates.

First MIT Press Edition, 1987.

© 1996 Massachusetts Institute of Technology

This book was set by the authors and was printed and bound in the United States of America.

Library of Congress Cataloging-in-Publication Data

Friedman, Daniel P.
   The little schemer / Daniel P. Friedman and Matthias Felleisen; drawings by Duane Bibby; foreword by Gerald J. Sussman.—4 ed., 1st MIT Press ed.
        p.   cm.
   Rev. ed. of: The little LISPer. 3rd ed. ©1989.
   Includes index.
   ISBN-13: 978-0-262-56099-3 (pbk.: alk. paper)
   ISNB-10: 0-262-56099-2 (pbk.: alk. paper)
   1. Scheme (Computer program language) 2. LISP (Computer program language)
I. Felleisen, Matthias. II. Friedman, Daniel P. Little LISPer. III. Title.
QA76.73.S34F75   1996
005.13′3—dc20   95-39853
                                                              CIP

20 19 18 17 16 15 14 13

To Mary, Helga, and our children

((Contents)

Foreword

This foreword appeared in the second and third editions of *The Little LISPer*. We reprint it here with the permission of the author.

In 1967 I took an introductory course in photography. Most of the students (including me) came into that course hoping to learn how to be creative—to take pictures like the ones I admired by artists such as Edward Weston. On the first day the teacher patiently explained the long list of technical skills that he was going to teach us during the term. A key was Ansel Adams' "Zone System" for previsualizing the print values (blackness in the final print) in a photograph and how they derive from the light intensities in the scene. In support of this skill we had to learn the use of exposure meters to measure light intensities and the use of exposure time and development time to control the black level and the contrast in the image. This is in turn supported by even lower level skills such as loading film, developing and printing, and mixing chemicals. One must learn to ritualize the process of developing sensitive material so that one gets consistent results over many years of work. The first laboratory session was devoted to finding out that developer feels slippery and that fixer smells awful.

But what about creative composition? In order to be creative one must first gain control of the medium. One can not even begin to think about organizing a great photograph without having the skills to make it happen. In engineering, as in other creative arts, we must learn to do analysis to support our efforts in synthesis. One cannot build a beautiful and functional bridge without a knowledge of steel and dirt and considerable mathematical technique for using this knowledge to compute the properties of structures. Similarly, one cannot build a beautiful computer system without a deep understanding of how to "previsualize" the process generated by the procedures one writes.

Some photographers choose to use black-and-white 8×10 plates while others choose 35mm slides. Each has its advantages and disadvantages. Like photography, programming requires a choice of medium. Lisp is the medium of choice for people who enjoy free style and flexibility. Lisp was initially conceived as a theoretical vehicle for recursion theory and for symbolic algebra. It has developed into a uniquely powerful and flexible family of software development tools, providing wrap-around support for the rapid-prototyping of software systems. As with other languages, Lisp provides the glue for using a vast library of canned parts, produced by members of the user community. In Lisp, procedures are first-class data, to be passed as arguments, returned as values, and stored in data structures. This flexibility is valuable, but most importantly, it provides mechanisms for formalizing, naming, and saving the idioms—the common patterns of usage that are essential to engineering design. In addition, Lisp programs can easily manipulate the representations of Lisp programs—a feature that has encouraged the development of a vast structure of program synthesis and analysis tools, such as cross-referencers.

The Little LISPer is a unique approach to developing the skills underlying creative programming in Lisp. It painlessly packages, with considerable wit, much of the drill and practice that is necessary to learn the skills of constructing recursive processes and manipulating recursive data-structures. For the student of Lisp programming, *The Little LISPer* can perform the same service that Hanon's finger exercises or Czerny's piano studies perform for the student of piano.

Gerald J. Sussman
Cambridge, Massachusetts

Preface

To celebrate the twentieth anniversary of Scheme we revised *The Little LISPer* a third time, gave it the more accurate title *The Little Schemer*, and wrote a sequel: *The Seasoned Schemer*.

Programs accept data and produce data. Designing a program requires a thorough understanding of data; a good program reflects the shape of the data it deals with. Most collections of data, and hence most programs, are recursive. Recursion is the act of defining an object or solving a problem in terms of itself.

The goal of this book is to teach the reader to think recursively. Our first task is to decide which language to use to communicate this concept. There are three obvious choices: a natural language, such as English; formal mathematics; or a programming language. Natural languages are ambiguous, imprecise, and sometimes awkwardly verbose. These are all virtues for general communication, but something of a drawback for communicating concisely as precise a concept as recursion. The language of mathematics is the opposite of natural language: it can express powerful formal ideas with only a few symbols. Unfortunately, the language of mathematics is often cryptic and barely accessible without special training. The marriage of technology and mathematics presents us with a third, almost ideal choice: a programming language. We believe that programming languages are the best way to convey the concept of recursion. They share with mathematics the ability to give a formal meaning to a set of symbols. But unlike mathematics, programming languages can be directly experienced—you can take the programs in this book, observe their behavior, modify them, and experience the effect of these modifications.

Perhaps the best programming language for teaching recursion is Scheme. Scheme is inherently symbolic—the programmer does not have to think about the relationship between the symbols of his own language and the representations in the computer. Recursion is Scheme's natural computational mechanism; the primary programming activity is the creation of (potentially) recursive definitions. Scheme implementations are predominantly interactive—the programmer can immediately participate in and observe the behavior of his programs. And, perhaps most importantly for our lessons at the end of this book, there is a direct correspondence between the structure of Scheme programs and the data those programs manipulate.

Although Scheme can be described quite formally, understanding Scheme does not require a particularly mathematical inclination. In fact, *The Little Schemer* is based on lecture notes from a two-week "quickie" introduction to Scheme for students with no previous programming experience and an admitted dislike for anything mathematical. Many of these students were preparing for careers in public affairs. It is our belief that *writing programs recursively in Scheme is essentially simple pattern recognition.* Since our only concern is recursive programming, our treatment is limited to the whys and wherefores of just a few Scheme features: car, cdr, cons, eq?, null?, zero?, add1, sub1, number?, and, or, quote, lambda, define, and cond. Indeed, our language is an *idealized* Scheme.

The Little Schemer and *The Seasoned Schemer* will not introduce you to the practical world of programming, but a mastery of the concepts in these books provides a start toward understanding the nature of computation.

What You Need to Know to Read This Book

The reader must be comfortable reading English, recognizing numbers, and counting.

Acknowledgments

We are indebted to many people for their contributions and assistance throughout the development of the second and third editions of this book. We thank Bruce Duba, Kent Dybvig, Chris Haynes, Eugene Kohlbecker, Richard Salter, George Springer, Mitch Wand, and David S. Wise for countless discussions that influenced our thinking while conceiving this book. Ghassan Abbas, Charles Baker, David Boyer, Mike Dunn, Terry Falkenberg, Rob Friedman, John Gateley, Mayer Goldberg, Iqbal Khan, Julia Lawall, Jon Mendelsohn, John Nienart, Jeffrey D. Perotti, Ed Robertson, Anne Shpuntoff, Erich Smythe, Guy Steele, Todd Stein, and Larry Weisselberg provided many important comments on the drafts of the book. We especially want to thank Bob Filman for being such a thorough and uncompromising critic through several readings. Finally we wish to acknowledge Nancy Garrett, Peg Fletcher, and Bob Filman for contributing to the design and TEXery.

The fourth and latest edition greatly benefited from Dorai Sitaram's incredibly clever Scheme typesetting program SLATEX. Kent Dybvig's Chez Scheme made programming in Scheme a most pleasant experience. We gratefully acknowledge criticisms and suggestions from Shelaswau Bushnell, Richard Cobbe, David Combs, Peter Drake, Kent Dybvig, Rob Friedman, Steve Ganz, Chris Haynes, Erik Hilsdale, Eugene Kohlbecker, Shriram Krishnamurthi, Julia Lawall, Suzanne Menzel Collin McCurdy, John Nienart, Jon Rossie, Jonathan Sobel, George Springer, Guy Steele, John David Stone, Vikram Subramaniam, Mitch Wand, and Melissa Wingard-Phillips.

Guidelines for the Reader

Do not rush through this book. Read carefully; valuable hints are scattered throughout the text. Do not read the book in fewer than three sittings. Read systematically. If you do not *fully* understand one chapter, you will understand the next one even less. The questions are ordered by increasing difficulty; it will be hard to answer later ones if you cannot solve the earlier ones.

The book is a dialogue between you and us about interesting examples of Scheme programs. If you can, try the examples while you read. Schemes are readily available. While there are minor syntactic variations between different implementations of Scheme (primarily the spelling of particular names and the domain of specific functions), Scheme is basically the same throughout the world. To work with Scheme, you will need to define atom?, sub1, and add1. which we introduced in *The Little Schemer*:

```
(define atom?
  (lambda (x)
    (and (not (pair? x)) (not (null? x)))))
```

To find out whether your Scheme has the correct definition of atom?, try (atom? (quote ())) and make sure it returns #f. In fact, the material is also suited for modern Lisps such as Common Lisp. To work with Lisp, you will also have to add the function atom?:

```
(defun atom? (x)
  (not (listp x)))
```

Moreover, you may need to modify the programs slightly. Typically, the material requires only a few changes. Suggestions about how to try the programs in the book are provided in the framenotes. Framenotes preceded by "S:" concern Scheme, those by "L:" concern Common Lisp.

In chapter 4 we develop basic arithmetic from three operators: *add1*, *sub1*, and *zero?*. Since Scheme does not provide *add1* and *sub1*, you must define them using the built-in primitives for addition and subtraction. Therefore, to avoid a circularity, our basic arithmetic addition and subtraction must be written using different symbols: + and −, respectively.

We do not give any formal definitions in this book. We believe that you can form your own definitions and will thus remember them and understand them better than if we had written each one for you. But be sure you know and understand the *Laws* and *Commandments* thoroughly before passing them by. The key to learning Scheme is "pattern recognition." The *Commandments* point out the patterns that you will have already seen. Early in the book, some concepts are narrowed for simplicity; later, they are expanded and qualified. You should also know that, while everything in the book is Scheme, Scheme itself is more general and incorporates more than we could intelligibly cover in an introductory text. After you have mastered this book, you can read and understand more advanced and comprehensive books on Scheme.

We use a few notational conventions throughout the text, primarily changes in typeface for different classes of symbols. Variables and the names of primitive operations are in *italic*. Basic data, including numbers and representations of truth and falsehood, is set in sans serif. Keywords, i.e., **define**, **lambda**, **cond**, **else**, **and**, **or**, and **quote**, are in **boldface**. When you try the programs, you may ignore the typefaces but not the related framenotes. To highlight this role of typefaces, the programs in framenotes are set in a `typewriter` face. The typeface distinctions can be safely ignored until chapter 10, where we treat programs as data.

Finally, Webster defines "punctuation" as the act of punctuating; specifically, the act, practice, or system of using standardized marks in writing and printing to separate sentences or sentence elements or to make the meaning clearer. We have taken this definition literally and have abandoned some familiar uses of punctuation in order to make the meaning clearer. Specifically, we have dropped the use of punctuation in the left-hand column whenever the item that precedes such punctuation is a term in our programming language.

Food appears in many of our examples for two reasons. First, food is easier to visualize than abstract symbols. (This is not a good book to read while dieting.) We hope the choice of food will help you understand the examples and concepts we use. Second, we want to provide you with a little distraction. We know how frustrating the subject matter can be, and a little distraction will help you keep your sanity.

You are now ready to start. Good luck! We hope you will enjoy the challenges waiting for you on the following pages.

Bon appétit!

Daniel P. Friedman
Matthias Felleisen

The Little Schemer

1.
Toys

Is it true that this is an atom?
  atom[1]
	Yes,
	    because **atom** is a string of characters beginning with the letter **a**.

[1] L, S: (quote atom) or 'atom
"L:" and "S:" are described in the preface.

Is it true that this is an atom?
  turkey
	Yes,
	    because **turkey** is a string of characters beginning with a letter.

Is it true that this is an atom?
  1492
	Yes,
	    because **1492** is a string of digits.

Is it true that this is an atom?
  u
	Yes,
	    because **u** is a string of one character, which is a letter.

Is it true that this is an atom?
  *abc$
	Yes,
	    because *abc$ is a string of characters beginning with a letter or special character other than a left "(" or right ")" parenthesis.

Is it true that this is a list?
  (atom)[1]
	Yes,
	    because **(atom)** is an atom enclosed by parentheses.

[1] L, S: (quote (atom)) or '(atom)

Is it true that this is a list?
  (atom turkey or)
	Yes,
	    because it is a collection of atoms enclosed by parentheses.

Is it true that this is a list?
    (atom turkey) or
	No,
	    because these are actually two
	    S-expressions not enclosed by parentheses.
	    The first one is a list containing two
	    atoms, and the second one is an atom.

Is it true that this is a list?
    ((atom turkey) or)
	Yes,
	    because the two S-expressions are now
	    enclosed by parentheses.

Is it true that this is an S-expression?
    xyz
	Yes,
	    because all atoms are S-expressions.

Is it true that this is an S-expression?
    (x y z)
	Yes,
	    because it is a list.

Is it true that this is an S-expression?
    ((x y) z)
	Yes,
	    because all lists are S-expressions.

Is it true that this is a list?
    (how are you doing so far)
	Yes,
	    because it is a collection of S-expressions
	    enclosed by parentheses.

How many S-expressions are in the list
    (how are you doing so far)
and what are they?
	Six,
	    how, are, you, doing, so, and far.

Is it true that this is a list?
    (((how) are) ((you) (doing so)) far)
	Yes,
	    because it is a collection of S-expressions
	    enclosed by parentheses.

How many S-expressions are in the list
    (((how) are) ((you) (doing so)) far)
and what are they?
	Three,
	    ((how) are), ((you) (doing so)), and far.

Is it true that this is a list?	Yes,
()	because it contains zero S-expressions enclosed by parentheses. This special S-expression is called the null (or empty) list.

Is it true that this is an atom?	No,
()	because () is just a list.

Is it true that this is a list?	Yes,
(() () () ())	because it is a collection of S-expressions enclosed by parentheses.

What is the *car* of l where l is the argument (a b c)	a, because a is the first atom of this list.

What is the *car* of l where l is ((a b c) x y z)	(a b c), because (a b c) is the first S-expression of this non-empty list.

What is the *car* of l where l is hotdog	No answer. You cannot ask for the *car* of an atom.

What is the *car* of l where l is ()	No answer.[1] You cannot ask for the *car* of the empty list.

---

[1] L: nil

The Law of Car

The primitive *car* is defined only for non-empty lists.

What is the *car* of *l*
where
    l is (((hotdogs)) (and) (pickle) relish)
	((hotdogs)),
	    read as:
	      "The list of the list of hotdogs."
	  ((hotdogs)) is the first S-expression of *l*.

What is (*car l*)
where
    l is (((hotdogs)) (and) (pickle) relish)
	((hotdogs)),
	    because (*car l*) is another way to ask for
	  "the *car* of the list *l*."

What is (*car* (*car l*)) where *l* is (((hotdogs)) (and))	(hotdogs).

What is the *cdr* of *l*
where
    l is (a b c)
 	
  Note: "cdr" is pronounced "could-er."
	(b c),
	    because (b c) is the list *l* without (*car l*).

What is the *cdr* of *l* where *l* is ((a b c) x y z)	(x y z).
What is the *cdr* of *l* where *l* is (hamburger)	().

What is (*cdr l*)
where
    l is ((x) t r)
	(t r),
	    because (*cdr l*) is just another way to ask
	  for "the cdr of the list *l*."

What is (*cdr a*)
where
    a is hotdogs
	No answer.
	    You cannot ask for the *cdr* of an atom.

What is (*cdr l*) where *l* is ()	No answer.[1] You cannot ask for the *cdr* of the null list.

<hr>

[1] L: nil

<hr>

The Law of Cdr

The primitive *cdr* is defined only for non-empty lists. The *cdr* of any non-empty list is always another list.

What is (*car* (*cdr l*))
where
  l is ((b) (x y) ((c)))
	(x y),
	  because ((x y) ((c))) is (*cdr l*), and (x y) is
	  the *car* of (*cdr l*).

What is (*cdr* (*cdr l*))
where
  l is ((b) (x y) ((c)))
	(((c))),
	  because ((x y) ((c))) is (*cdr l*), and (((c)))
	  is the *cdr* of (*cdr l*).

What is (*cdr* (*car l*))
where
  l is (a (b (c)) d)
	No answer,
	  since (*car l*) is an atom, and *cdr* does not
	  take an atom as an argument; see The Law
	  of Cdr.

What does *car* take as an argument?	It takes any non-empty list.
What does *cdr* take as an argument?	It takes any non-empty list.

What is the *cons* of the atom *a* and the list *l*
where *a* is peanut
and
  l is (butter and jelly)
This can also be written "(*cons a l*)".
  Read: "*cons* the atom *a* onto the list *l*."
	(peanut butter and jelly),
	  because *cons* adds an atom to the front of
	  a list.

What is the *cons* of *s* and *l*
 where *s* is (banana and)
 and
     l is (peanut butter and jelly)
	((banana and) peanut butter and jelly),
	     because *cons* adds any S-expression to the
	     front of a list.

What is (*cons s l*)
 where
     s is ((help) this)
 and
     l is (is very ((hard) to learn))
	(((help) this) is very ((hard) to learn)).

What does *cons* take as its arguments?	*cons* takes two arguments:
	     the first one is any S-expression;
	     the second one is any list.

What is (*cons s l*)
 where
     s is (a b (c))
 and
     l is ()
	((a b (c))),
	     because () is a list.

What is (*cons s l*) where *s* is a and *l* is ()	(a).

What is (*cons s l*)
 where
     s is ((a b c))
 and
     l is b
	No answer,[1]
	     since the second argument *l* must be a list.

What is (*cons s l*) where *s* is a and *l* is b	No answer. Why?

---

[1] In practice, (cons α β) works for all values α and β, and
    (car (cons α β)) = α
    (cdr (cons α β)) = β.

The Law of Cons

The primitive *cons* takes two arguments. The second argument to *cons* must be a list. The result is a list.

What is (*cons s* (*car l*)) where *s* is **a** and *l* is ((b) c d)	(a b). Why?

What is (*cons s* (*cdr l*)) where *s* is **a** and *l* is ((b) c d)	(a c d). Why?

Is it true that the list *l* is the null list where *l* is ()	Yes, because it is the list composed of zero S-expressions. This question can also be written: (*null? l*).

What is (*null?*[1] (**quote** ()))	True, because (**quote** ())[1] is a notation for the null list.

---

[1] L: null

[1] L: Also () and '(). S: Also '().

Is (*null? l*) true or false where *l* is (a b c)	False, because *l* is a non-empty list.

Is (*null?* *a*) true or false where
   a is spaghetti
	No answer,[1]
	   because you cannot ask *null?* of an atom.

<hr>

[1] In practice, (`null?` α) is false for everything, except the empty list.

<hr>

The Law of Null?

The primitive *null?* is defined only for lists.

<hr>

Is it true or false that *s* is an atom where *s* is Harry	True, because Harry is a string of characters beginning with a letter.

Is (*atom?*[1] *s*) true or false where
   s is Harry
	True,
	   because (*atom?* *s*) is just another way to ask "Is *s* is an atom?"

<hr>

[1] L: (defun atom? (x)
      (not (listp x)))
  S: (define atom?
     (lambda (x)
      (and (not (pair? x)) (not (null? x)))))

<hr>

Is (*atom?* *s*) true or false where
   s is (Harry had a heap of apples)
	False,
	   since *s* is a list.

How many arguments does *atom?* take and what are they?	It takes one argument. The argument can be any S-expression.

Is $(atom?\ (car\ l))$ true or false
where
    l is (Harry had a heap of apples)
	True,
	    because $(car\ l)$ is Harry, and Harry is an
	    atom.

Is $(atom?\ (cdr\ l))$ true or false where l is (Harry had a heap of apples)	False.

Is $(atom?\ (cdr\ l))$ true or false
where
    l is (Harry)
	False,
	    because the list () is not an atom.

Is $(atom?\ (car\ (cdr\ l)))$ true or false
where
    l is (swing low sweet cherry oat)
	True,
	    because $(cdr\ l)$ is (low sweet cherry oat),
	    and $(car\ (cdr\ l))$ is low, which is an atom.

Is $(atom?\ (car\ (cdr\ l)))$ true or false
where
    l is (swing (low sweet) cherry oat)
	False,
	    since $(cdr\ l)$ is ((low sweet) cherry oat), and
	    $(car\ (cdr\ l))$ is (low sweet), which is a list.

True or false: $a1$ and $a2$ are the same atom
where $a1$ is Harry
and
    $a2$ is Harry
	True,
	    because $a1$ is the atom Harry and $a2$ is the
	    atom Harry.

Is $(eq?^{[1]}\ a1\ a2)$ true or false
where $a1$ is Harry
and
    $a2$ is Harry
	True,
	    because $(eq?\ a1\ a2)$ is just another way to
	    ask, "Are $a1$ and $a2$ the same
	    non-numeric atom?"

[1] L: eq

Is $(eq?\ a1\ a2)$ true or false
where $a1$ is margarine
and
    $a2$ is butter
	False,
	    since $a1$ and $a2$ are different atoms.

How many arguments does *eq?* take and what are they?	It takes two arguments. Both of them must be non-numeric atoms.
Is (*eq? l1 l2*) true or false where *l1* is () and *l2* is (strawberry)	No answer,[1] () and (strawberry) are lists.

<hr>

[1] In practice, lists may be arguments of **eq?**. Two lists are **eq?** if they are the same list.

Is (*eq? n1 n2*) true or false where *n1* is 6 and *n2* is 7	No answer,[1] 6 and 7 are numbers.

<hr>

[1] In practice, some numbers may be arguments of **eq?**.

The Law of Eq?

The primitive *eq?* takes two arguments. Each must be a non-numeric atom.

Is (*eq?* (*car l*) *a*) true or false where *l* is (Mary had a little lamb chop) and *a* is Mary	True, because (*car l*) is the atom Mary, and the argument *a* is also the atom Mary.
Is (*eq?* (*cdr l*) *a*) true or false where *l* is (soured milk) and *a* is milk	No answer. See The Laws of Eq? and Cdr.

Is ($eq?$ ($car\ l$) (car ($cdr\ l$))) true or false
where
   l is (beans beans we need jelly beans)

True,
   because it compares the first and second
   atoms in the list.

$\Rightarrow$ **Now go make yourself a peanut butter and jelly sandwich.** $\Leftarrow$

This space reserved for

JELLY STAINS!

2.
Do It, Do It Again, and Again, and Again...

True or false: (*lat? l*)
where
    l is (Jack Sprat could eat no chicken fat)
	True,
	    because each S-expression in *l* is an atom.

True or false: (*lat? l*)
where
    l is ((Jack) Sprat could eat no chicken fat)
	False,
	    since (*car l*) is a list.

True or false: (*lat? l*)
where
    l is (Jack (Sprat could) eat no chicken fat)
	False,
	    since one of the S-expressions in *l* is a list.

True or false: (*lat? l*) where *l* is ()	True, because it does not contain a list.
True or false: a lat is a list of atoms.	True! Every lat is a list of atoms!
Write the function *lat?* using some, but not necessarily all, of the following functions: *car cdr cons null? atom?* and *eq?*	You were not expected to be able to do this yet, because you are still missing some ingredients. Go on to the next question. Good luck.

Are you rested?

```
(define lat?¹
  (lambda (l)
    (cond
      ((null? l) #t )
      ((atom? (car l)) (lat? (cdr l)))
      (else #f ))))
```

What is the value of (*lat? l*)
where
  l is the argument (bacon and eggs)

#t .
  The application (*lat? l*)
  where
    l is (bacon and eggs)
  has the value #t —true—because *l* is a lat.

---

[1] L: (defun lat? (l)
    (cond
      ((null l) t)
      ((atom? (car l)) (lat? (cdr l)))
      (t nil)))

How do we determine the answer #t for the
application
  (*lat? l*)

You were not expected to know this one
either. The answer is determined by
answering the questions asked by *lat?*
  Hint: Write down the definition of the
  function *lat?* and refer to it for the next
  group of questions.

What is the first question asked by (*lat? l*)

(*null? l*)
  Note:
    (**cond** ...) asks questions;
    (**lambda** ...) creates a function; and
    (**define** ...) gives it a name.

What is the meaning of the **cond**-line
  ((*null? l*) #t)
where
  l is (bacon and eggs)

(*null? l*) asks if the argument *l* is the null
list. If it is, the value of the application is
true. If it is not, we ask the next question.
In this case, *l* is not the null list, so we ask
the next question.

What is the next question?

(*atom? (car l)*).

What is the meaning of the line
  $((atom?\ (car\ l))\ (lat?\ (cdr\ l)))$
where
  l is (bacon and eggs)
	$(atom?\ (car\ l))$ asks if the first S-expression of the list l is an atom. If $(car\ l)$ is an atom, we want to know if the rest of l is also composed only of atoms. If $(car\ l)$ is not an atom, we ask the next question. In this case, $(car\ l)$ is an atom, so the value of the function is the value of $(lat?\ (cdr\ l))$.

What is the meaning of $(lat?\ (cdr\ l))$	$(lat?\ (cdr\ l))$ finds out if the rest of the list l is composed only of atoms, by referring to the function with a new argument.
Now what is the argument l for $lat?$	Now the argument l is $(cdr\ l)$, which is (and eggs).
What is the next question?	$(null?\ l)$.

What is the meaning of the line
  $((null?\ l)\ \#t\ )$
where
  l is now (and eggs)
	$(null?\ l)$ asks if the argument l is the null list. If it is, the value of the application is $\#t$. If it is not, we ask the next question. In this case, l is not the null list, so we ask the next question.

What is the next question?	$(atom?\ (car\ l))$.

What is the meaning of the line
  $((atom?\ (car\ l))\ (lat?\ (cdr\ l)))$
where
  l is (and eggs)
	$(atom?\ (car\ l))$ asks if $(car\ l)$ is an atom. If it is an atom, the value of the application is $(lat?\ (cdr\ l))$. If not, we ask the next question. In this case, $(car\ l)$ is an atom, so we want to find out if the rest of the list l is composed only of atoms.

What is the meaning of $(lat?\ (cdr\ l))$	$(lat?\ (cdr\ l))$ finds out if the rest of l is composed only of atoms, by referring again to the function $lat?$, but this time, with the argument $(cdr\ l)$, which is (eggs).

What is the next question?	*(null? l)*.

What is the meaning of the line
    ((*null? l*) #t)
where
    l is now (eggs)
	(*null? l*) asks if the argument *l* is the null list. If it is, the value of the application is #t —true. If it is not, move to the next question. In this case, *l* is not null, so we ask the next question.

What is the next question?	*(atom? (car l))*.

What is the meaning of the line
    ((*atom? (car l)*) (*lat? (cdr l)*))
where
    l is now (eggs)
	(*atom? (car l)*) asks if (*car l*) is an atom. If it is, the value of the application is (*lat? (cdr l)*). If (*car l*) is not an atom, ask the next question. In this case, (*car l*) is an atom, so once again we look at (*lat? (cdr l)*).

What is the meaning of (*lat? (cdr l)*)	(*lat? (cdr l)*) finds out if the rest of the list *l* is composed only of atoms, by referring to the function *lat?*, with *l* becoming the value of (*cdr l*).

Now, what is the argument for *lat?*	().

What is the meaning of the line
    ((*null? l*) #t)
where
    l is now ()
	(*null? l*) asks if the argument *l* is the null list. If it is, the value of the application is the value of #t . If not, we ask the next question. In this case, () is the null list. So, the value of the application (*lat? l*)
	where
	    l is (bacon and eggs), is #t —true.

Do you remember the question about
    (*lat? l*)
	Probably not. The application (*lat? l*) has the value #t if the list *l* is a list of atoms where
	    l is (bacon and eggs).

Can you describe what the function *lat?* does in your own words?

Here are our words:

"*lat?* looks at each S-expression in a list, in turn, and asks if each S-expression is an atom, until it runs out of S-expressions. If it runs out without encountering a list, the value is #t. If it finds a list, the value is #f—false."

To see how we could arrive at a value of "false," consider the next few questions.

This is the function *lat?* again:

```
(define lat?
  (lambda (l)
    (cond
      ((null? l) #t)
      ((atom? (car l)) (lat? (cdr l)))
      (else #f))))
```

What is the value of (*lat?* *l*)
where
   l is now (bacon (and eggs))

#f,
   since the list *l* contains an S-expression that is a list.

What is the first question?

(*null?* *l*).

What is the meaning of the line
   ((*null?* *l*) #t)
where
   l is (bacon (and eggs))

(*null?* *l*) asks if *l* is the null list. If it is, the value is #t. If *l* is not null, move to the next question. In this case, it is not null, so we ask the next question.

What is the next question?

(*atom?* (*car* *l*)).

What is the meaning of the line
   ((*atom?* (*car* *l*)) (*lat?* (*cdr* *l*)))
where
   l is (bacon (and eggs))

(*atom?* (*car* *l*)) asks if (*car* *l*) is an atom. If it is, the value is (*lat?* (*cdr* *l*)). If it is not, we ask the next question. In this case, (*car* *l*) is an atom, so we want to check if the rest of the list *l* is composed only of atoms.

Do It, Do It Again, and Again, and Again ...

19

What is the meaning of (*lat?* (*cdr l*))	(*lat?* (*cdr l*)) checks to see if the rest of the list *l* is composed only of atoms, by referring to *lat?* with *l* replaced by (*cdr l*).

What is the meaning of the line
    ((*null? l*) #t)
where
    l is now ((and eggs))
	(*null? l*) asks if *l* is the null list. If it is null, the value is #t. If it is not null, we ask the next question. In this case, *l* is not null, so move to the next question.

What is the next question?	(*atom?* (*car l*)).

What is the meaning of the line
    ((*atom?* (*car l*)) (*lat?* (*cdr l*)))
where
    l is now ((and eggs))
	(*atom?* (*car l*)) asks if (*car l*) is an atom. If it is, the value is (*lat?* (*cdr l*)). If it is not, we move to the next question. In this case, (*car l*) is not an atom, so we ask the next question.

What is the next question?	**else**.
What is the meaning of the question **else**	**else** asks if **else** is true.
Is **else** true?	Yes, because the question **else** is always true!
else	Of course.
Why is **else** the last question?	Because we do not need to ask any more questions.
Why do we not need to ask any more questions?	Because a list can be empty, can have an atom in the first position, or can have a list in the first position.
What is the meaning of the line (**else** #f)	**else** asks if **else** is true. If **else** is true—as it always is—then the answer is #f—false.

What is)))	These are the closing or matching parentheses of (**cond** ..., (**lambda** ..., and (**define** ..., which appear at the beginning of a function definition.

Can you describe how we determined the value #f for
    (*lat? l*)
where
    l is (bacon (and eggs))
	Here is one way to say it:
	"(*lat? l*) looks at each item in its argument to see if it is an atom. If it runs out of items before it finds a list, the value of (*lat? l*) is #t. If it finds a list, as it did in the example (bacon (and eggs)), the value of (*lat? l*) is #f."

Is (**or** (*null? l1*) (*atom? l2*)) true or false
where *l1* is ()
and
    l2 is (d e f g)
	True,
	    because (*null? l1*) is true where *l1* is ().

Is (**or** (*null? l1*) (*null? l2*)) true or false
where
    l1 is (a b c)
and
    l2 is ()
	True,
	    because (*null? l2*) is true where *l2* is ().

Is (**or** (*null? l1*) (*null? l2*)) true or false
where
    l1 is (a b c)
and
    l2 is (atom)
	False,
	    because neither (*null? l1*) nor (*null? l2*) is true where
	        l1 is (a b c)
	    and
	        l2 is (atom).

What does (**or** ...) do?	(**or** ...) asks two questions, one at a time. If the first one is true it stops and answers true. Otherwise it asks the second question and answers with whatever the second question answers.

| Is it true or false that *a* is a member of *lat* where *a* is **tea** and *lat* is (**coffee tea or milk**) | True, because one of the atoms of the lat, (**coffee tea or milk**) is the same as the atom *a*—**tea**. |

| Is (*member? a lat*) true or false where *a* is **poached** and *lat* is (**fried eggs and scrambled eggs**) | False, since *a* is not one of the atoms of the lat. |

This is the function *member?*

```
(define member?
  (lambda (a lat)
    (cond
      ((null? lat) #f)
      (else (or (eq? (car lat) a)
                (member? a (cdr lat)))))))
```

What is the value of (*member? a lat*)
where *a* is **meat**
and
    lat is (**mashed potatoes and meat gravy**)

#t ,
    because the atom **meat** is one of the atoms
    of *lat*,
        (**mashed potatoes and meat gravy**).

| How do we determine the value #t for the above application? | The value is determined by asking the questions about (*member? a lat*). Hint: Write down the definition of the function *member?* and refer to it while you work on the next group of questions. |

| What is the first question asked by (*member? a lat*) | (*null? lat*). This is also the first question asked by *lat?*. |

The First Commandment

(preliminary)

Always ask *null?* **as the first question in expressing any function.**

What is the meaning of the line
   ((*null?* *lat*) #f)
where
   lat is (mashed potatoes and meat gravy)

(*null?* *lat*) asks if *lat* is the null list. If it is, the value is #f, since the atom **meat** was not found in *lat*. If not, we ask the next question. In this case, it is not null, so we ask the next question.

What is the next question?

else.

Why is **else** the next question?

Because we do not need to ask any more questions.

Is **else** really a question?

Yes, **else** is a question whose value is always true.

What is the meaning of the line
   (**else** (**or** (*eq?* (*car lat*) *a*)
        (*member?* *a* (*cdr lat*))))

Now that we know that *lat* is not *null?*, we have to find out whether the *car* of *lat* is the same atom as *a*, or whether *a* is somewhere in the rest of *lat*. The answer
   (**or** (*eq?* (*car lat*) *a*)
       (*member?* *a* (*cdr lat*)))
does this.

True or false:
   (**or** (*eq?* (*car lat*) *a*)
     (*member?* *a* (*cdr lat*)))
where *a* is **meat**
and
   lat is (mashed potatoes and meat gravy)

We will find out by looking at each question in turn.

Is (*eq?* (*car lat*) *a*) true or false
where *a* is meat
and
    lat is (mashed potatoes and meat gravy)
	False,
	    because meat is not *eq?* to mashed,
	    the *car* of
	        (mashed potatoes and meat gravy).

What is the second question of (**or** ...)	(*member? a* (*cdr lat*)).
	    This refers to the function with the
	    argument *lat* replaced by (*cdr lat*).

Now what are the arguments of *member?*	*a* is meat
	and
	    lat is now (*cdr lat*), specifically
	    (potatoes and meat gravy).

What is the next question?	(*null? lat*). Remember The First Commandment.
Is (*null? lat*) true or false where *lat* is (potatoes and meat gravy)	#f—false.
What do we do now?	Ask the next question.
What is the next question?	**else**.

What is the meaning of
    (**or** (*eq?* (*car lat*) *a*)
        (*member? a* (*cdr lat*)))
	(**or** (*eq?* (*car lat*) *a*)
	    (*member? a* (*cdr lat*)))
	finds out if *a* is *eq?* to the *car* of *lat* or if *a* is
	a member of the *cdr* of *lat* by referring to the
	function.

Is *a* *eq?* to the *car* of *lat*	No, because *a* is meat and the *car* of *lat* is potatoes.

So what do we do next?	We ask (*member? a* (*cdr lat*)).
Now, what are the arguments of *member?*	*a* is meat, and *lat* is (and meat gravy).
What is the next question?	(*null? lat*).
What do we do now?	Ask the next question, since (*null? lat*) is false.
What is the next question?	**else**.

What is the value of
  (**or** (*eq?* (*car lat*) *a*)
    (*member? a* (*cdr lat*)))
	The value of (*member? a* (*cdr lat*)).

Why?	Because (*eq?* (*car lat*) *a*) is false.
What do we do now?	Recur—refer to the function with new arguments.
What are the new arguments?	*a* is meat, and *lat* is (meat gravy).
What is the next question?	(*null? lat*).
What do we do now?	Since (*null? lat*) is false, ask the next question.
What is the next question?	**else**.

What is the value of
    (**or** (*eq?* (*car lat*) *a*)
      (*member?* *a* (*cdr lat*)))
	#t ,
	because (*car lat*), which is meat, and *a*,
	which is meat, are the same atom.
	Therefore, (**or** ...) answers with #t .

What is the value of the application
    (*member?* *a lat*)
where *a* is meat
and
    lat is (meat gravy)
	#t ,
	because we have found that meat is a
	member of
	    (meat gravy).

What is the value of the application
    (*member?* *a lat*)
where *a* is meat
and
    lat is (and meat gravy)
	#t ,
	because meat is also a member of the *lat*
	    (and meat gravy).

What is the value of the application
    (*member?* *a lat*)
where *a* is meat
and
    lat is (potatoes and meat gravy)
	#t ,
	because meat is also a member of the *lat*
	    (potatoes and meat gravy).

What is the value of the application
    (*member?* *a lat*)
where *a* is meat
and
    lat is (mashed potatoes and meat gravy)
	#t ,
	because meat is also a member of the *lat*
	    (mashed potatoes and meat gravy).
	Of course, this is our original *lat*.

Just to make sure you have it right, let's
quickly run through it again. What is the
value of (*member?* *a lat*)
where
    a is meat
and
    lat is (mashed potatoes and meat gravy)
	#t .
	Hint: Write down the definition of the
	function *member?* and its arguments and
	refer to them as you go through the next
	group of questions.

(*null? lat*)	No. Move to the next line.

else	Yes.
(**or** (*eq?* (*car lat*) *a*) (*member?* *a* (*cdr lat*)))	Perhaps.
(*eq?* (*car lat*) *a*)	No. Ask the next question.
What next?	Recur with *a* and (*cdr lat*) where *a* is meat and (*cdr lat*) is (potatoes and meat gravy).
(*null? lat*)	No. Move to the next line.

else	Yes, but (*eq?* (*car lat*) *a*) is false.
	   Recur with *a* and (*cdr lat*)
	   where *a* is meat
	   and
	      (*cdr lat*) is (and meat gravy).

(*null? lat*)	No. Move to the next line.

else	Yes, but (*eq?* (*car lat*) *a*) is false.
	   Recur with *a* and (*cdr lat*)
	   where *a* is meat
	   and
	      (*cdr lat*) is (meat gravy).

(*null? lat*)	No. Move to the next line.
(*eq?* (*car lat*) *a*)	Yes, the value is #t .

(**or** (*eq?* (*car lat*) *a*) (*member? a* (*cdr lat*)))	#t.

What is the value of (*member? a lat*) where *a* is meat and *lat* is (meat gravy)	#t.

What is the value of (*member? a lat*) where *a* is meat and *lat* is (and meat gravy)	#t.

What is the value of (*member? a lat*) where *a* is meat and *lat* is (potatoes and meat gravy)	#t.

What is the value of (*member? a lat*) where *a* is meat and *lat* is (mashed potatoes and meat gravy)	#t.

What is the value of (*member? a lat*) where *a* is liver and *lat* is (bagels and lox)	#f.

Let's work out why it is #f. What's the first question *member?* asks?	(*null? lat*).

(*null? lat*)	No. Move to the next line.

else	Yes, but (*eq?* (*car lat*) *a*) is false. Recur with *a* and (*cdr lat*) where *a* is liver and (*cdr lat*) is (and lox).
(*null? lat*)	No. Move to the next line.
else	Yes, but (*eq?* (*car lat*) *a*) is false. Recur with *a* and (*cdr lat*) where *a* is liver and (*cdr lat*) is (lox).
(*null? lat*)	No. Move to the next line.
else	Yes, but (*eq?* (*car lat*) *a*) is still false. Recur with *a* and (*cdr lat*) where *a* is liver and (*cdr lat*) is ().
(*null? lat*)	Yes.
What is the value of (*member? a lat*) where *a* is liver and *lat* is ()	#f.

What is the value of
   (**or** (*eq?* (*car lat*) *a*)
    (*member? a* (*cdr lat*))))
where
   a is liver
and
   lat is (lox)
	#f.

What is the value of (*member? a lat*)
where *a* is liver
and
   lat is (lox)

                                            #f.

What is the value of
   (**or** (*eq? (car lat) a*)
     (*member? a (cdr lat)*)))
where
   a is liver
and
   lat is (and lox)

                                            #f.

What is the value of (*member? a lat*)
where *a* is liver
and
   lat is (and lox)

                                            #f.

What is the value of
   (**or** (*eq? (car lat) a*)
     (*member? a (cdr lat)*)))
where
   a is liver
and
   lat is (bagels and lox)

                                            #f.

What is the value of (*member? a lat*)
where *a* is liver
and
   lat is (bagels and lox)

                                            #f.

Do you believe all this? Then you may rest!

This space for doodling

3.
Cons the Magnificent

What is (*rember a lat*) where *a* is mint and *lat* is (lamb chops and mint jelly)	(lamb chops and jelly) "Rember" stands for *rem*ove a mem*ber*.

(*rember a lat*)
where *a* is mint
and
   lat is (lamb chops and
      mint flavored mint jelly)
	(lamb chops and flavored mint jelly).

(*rember a lat*) where *a* is toast and *lat* is (bacon lettuce and tomato)	(bacon lettuce and tomato).
(*rember a lat*) where *a* is cup and *lat* is (coffee cup tea cup and hick cup)	(coffee tea cup and hick cup).
What does (*rember a lat*) do?	It takes an atom and a lat as its arguments, and makes a new lat with the first occurrence of the atom in the old lat removed.
What steps should we use to do this?	First we will test (*null? lat*)—The First Commandment.
And if (*null? lat*) is true?	Return ().
What do we know if (*null? lat*) is not true?	We know that there must be at least one atom in the lat.
Is there any other question we should ask about the lat?	No. Either a lat is empty or it contains at least one atom.

What do we do if we know that the lat contains at least one atom?	We ask whether a is equal to $(car\ lat)$.

How do we ask questions?	By using
	(**cond**
	  (——— ———)
	  (——— ———)).

How do we ask if a is the same as $(car\ lat)$	$(eq?\ (car\ lat)\ a)$.

What would be the value of $(rember\ a\ lat)$ if a were the same as $(car\ lat)$	$(cdr\ lat)$.

What do we do if a is not the same as $(car\ lat)$	We want to keep $(car\ lat)$, but also find out if a is somewhere in the rest of the lat.

How do we remove the first occurrence of a in the rest of lat	$(rember\ a\ (cdr\ lat))$.

Is there any other question we should ask?	No.

Now, let's write down what we have so far:

```
(define rember
  (lambda (a lat)
    (cond
      ((null? lat) (quote ()))
      (else (cond
              ((eq? (car lat) a) (cdr lat))
              (else (rember a
                      (cdr lat)))))))))
```

What is the value of $(rember\ a\ lat)$ where
  a is bacon
and
  lat is (bacon lettuce and tomato)

(lettuce and tomato).
  Hint: Write down the function $rember$ and its arguments, and refer to them as you go through the next sequence of questions.

Now, let's see if this function works. What is the first question?	(*null? lat*).
What do we do now?	Move to the next line and ask the next question.
else	Yes.
What next?	Ask the next question.
(*eq?* (*car lat*) a)	Yes, so the value is (*cdr lat*). In this case, it is the list (lettuce and tomato).
Is this the correct value?	Yes, because it is the original list without the atom **bacon**.
But did we really use a good example?	Who knows? But the proof of the pudding is in the eating, so let's try another example.
What does *rember* do?	It takes an atom and a lat as its arguments, and makes a new lat with the first occurrence of the atom in the old lat removed.
What do we do now?	We compare each atom of the lat with the atom *a*, and if the comparison fails we build a list that begins with the atom we just compared.
What is the value of (*rember a lat*) where *a* is and and *lat* is (bacon lettuce and tomato)	(bacon lettuce tomato).

Let us see if our function *rember* works. What is the first question asked by *rember*	(*null? lat*).
What do we do now?	Move to the next line, and ask the next question.
else	Okay, so ask the next question.
(*eq?* (*car lat*) a)	No, so move to the next line.

What is the meaning of (**else** (*rember a* (*cdr lat*)))	**else** asks if **else** is true—as it always is—and the rest of the line says to recur with *a* and (*cdr lat*), where
	    a is and
	and
	    (*cdr lat*) is (lettuce and tomato).

(*null? lat*)	No, so move to the next line.
else	Sure.
(*eq?* (*car lat*) a)	No, so move to the next line.

What is the meaning of (*rember a* (*cdr lat*))	Recur
	where
	    a is and
	and
	    (*cdr lat*) is (and tomato).

(*null? lat*)	No, so move to the next line, and ask the next question.
else	Of course.

(eq? (car lat) a)	Yes.
So what is the result?	*(cdr lat)*—(tomato).
Is this correct?	No, since (tomato) is not the list (bacon lettuce and tomato) with just *a*—and—removed.
What did we do wrong?	We dropped and, but we also lost all the atoms preceding and.
How can we keep from losing the atoms bacon and lettuce	We use Cons the Magnificent. Remember *cons*, from chapter 1?

The Second Commandment

Use *cons* to build lists.

Let's see what happens when we use *cons*

```
(define rember
  (lambda (a lat)
    (cond
      ((null? lat) (quote ()))
      (else (cond
              ((eq? (car lat) a) (cdr lat))
              (else (cons (car lat)
                      (rember a
                        (cdr lat)))))))))
```

What is the value of *(rember a lat)*
where *a* is and
and
  lat is (bacon lettuce and tomato)

(bacon lettuce tomato).
  Hint: Make a copy of this function with *cons* and the arguments *a* and *lat* so you can refer to it for the following questions.

What is the first question?	(*null? lat*).
What do we do now?	Ask the next question.
else	Yes, of course.
(*eq? (car lat) a*)	No, so move to the next line.

What is the meaning of
  (*cons (car lat)*
    (*rember a*
      (*cdr lat*)))
where
  a is and
and
  lat is (bacon lettuce and tomato)
	It says to *cons* the *car* of *lat*—bacon—onto
	the value of
	  (*rember a (cdr lat*)).
	But since we don't know the value of
	(*rember a (cdr lat*)) yet, we must find it
	before we can *cons (car lat*) onto it.

What is the meaning of (*rember a (cdr lat*))	This refers to the function with *lat* replaced by (*cdr lat*)—(lettuce and tomato).
(*null? lat*)	No, so move to the next line.
else	Yes, ask the next question.
(*eq? (car lat) a*)	No, so move to the next line.

What is the meaning of
  (*cons (car lat)*
    (*rember a*
      (*cdr lat*)))
	It says to *cons* the *car* of *lat*—lettuce—onto
	the value of
	  (*rember a (cdr lat*)).
	But since we don't know the value of
	(*rember a (cdr lat*)) yet, we must find it
	before we can *cons (car lat*) onto it.

What is the meaning of (*rember a* (*cdr lat*))	This refers to the function with *lat* replaced by (*cdr lat*), that is, (and tomato).
(*null? lat*)	No, so ask the next question.
else	Still.
(*eq?* (*car lat*) *a*)	Yes.
What is the value of the line ((*eq?* (*car lat*) *a*) (*cdr lat*))	(*cdr lat*)—(tomato).

Are we finished?	Certainly not! We know what (*rember a lat*) is when *lat* is (and tomato), but we don't yet know what it is when *lat* is
	   (lettuce and tomato)
	or
	   (bacon lettuce and tomato).

We now have a value for
   (*rember a* (*cdr lat*))
where *a* is and
and
   (*cdr lat*) is (and tomato)
This value is (tomato)
What next?
	Recall that we wanted to *cons* lettuce onto the value of (*rember a* (*cdr lat*))
	where
	   a was and and (*cdr lat*) was (and tomato).
	Now that we have this value, which is (tomato), we can *cons* lettuce onto it.

What is the result when we *cons* lettuce onto (tomato)	(lettuce tomato).

What does (lettuce tomato) represent?	It represents the value of
	   (*cons* (*car lat*)
	      (*rember a*
	         (*cdr lat*))),
	when
	   lat is (lettuce and tomato)
	and
	   (*rember a* (*cdr lat*)) is (tomato).

Are we finished yet?	Not quite. So far we know what
	(*rember a lat*) is when
	    lat is (lettuce and tomato),
	but we don't yet know what it is when
	    lat is (bacon lettuce and tomato).

We now have a value for (*rember a* (*cdr lat*))
where *a* is **and**
and
    (*cdr lat*) is (lettuce and tomato)
This value is (lettuce tomato)
This is not the final value, so what must we
do again?
	Recall that, at one time, we wanted to *cons*
	bacon onto the value of (*rember a* (*cdr lat*)),
	where
	    a was **and**
	and
	    (*cdr lat*) was (lettuce and tomato).
	Now that we have this value, which is
	    (lettuce tomato),
	we can *cons* bacon onto it.

What is the result when we *cons* bacon onto (lettuce tomato)	(bacon lettuce tomato).

What does (bacon lettuce tomato) represent?[†]	It represents the value of
	    (*cons* (*car lat*)
	        (*rember a* (*cdr lat*))),
	when
	    lat is (bacon lettuce and tomato)
	and
	    (*rember a* (*cdr lat*)) is (lettuce tomato).

[†] Lunch?

Are we finished yet?	Yes.

Can you put in your own words how we
determined the final value
    (bacon lettuce tomato)
	In our words:
	    "The function *rember* checked each atom of
	    the lat, one at a time, to see if it was the
	    same as the atom **and**. If the *car* was not
	    the same as the atom, we saved it to be
	    *cons*ed to the final value later. When
	    rember found the atom **and**, it dropped it,
	    and *cons*ed the previous atoms back onto
	    the rest of the lat."

Can you rewrite *rember* so that it reflects the above description?	Yes, we can simplify it.

```
(define rember
  (lambda (a lat)
    (cond
      ((null? lat) (quote ()))
      ((eq? (car lat) a) (cdr lat))
      (else (cons (car lat)
              (rember a (cdr lat)))))))
```

Do you think this is simpler?	Functions like *rember* can always be simplified in this manner.
So why don't we simplify right away?	Because then a function's structure does not coincide with its argument's structure.

Let's see if the new *rember* is the same as the old one. What is the value of the application
   (*rember a lat*)
 where *a* is and
 and
   lat is (bacon lettuce and tomato)
	(bacon lettuce tomato).
	   Hint: Write down the function *rember* and its arguments and refer to them as you go through the next sequence of questions.

(*null? lat*)	No.
(*eq?* (*car lat*) *a*)	No.

else	Yes, so the value is
	   (*cons* (*car lat*)
	     (*rember a* (*cdr lat*))).

What is the meaning of
   (*cons* (*car lat*)
     (*rember a* (*cdr lat*)))
	This says to refer to the function *rember* but with the argument *lat* replaced by (*cdr lat*), and that after we arrive at a value for (*rember a* (*cdr lat*)) we must *cons* (*car lat*)—bacon—onto it.

(*null? lat*)	No.
(*eq?* (*car lat*) *a*)	No.

else	Yes, so the value is
	    (*cons* (*car lat*)
	      (*rember a* (*cdr lat*))).

What is the meaning of
    (*cons* (*car lat*)
      (*rember a* (*cdr lat*)))
	This says we recur using the function *rember*, with the argument *lat* replaced by (*cdr lat*), and that after we arrive at a value for (*rember a* (*cdr lat*)), we must *cons* (*car lat*)—lettuce—onto it.

(*null? lat*)	No.
(*eq?* (*car lat*) *a*)	Yes.
What is the value of the line ((*eq?* (*car lat*) *a*) (*cdr lat*))	It is (*cdr lat*)—(tomato).
Now what?	Now *cons* (*car lat*)—lettuce—onto (tomato).
Now what?	Now *cons* (*car lat*)—bacon—onto (lettuce tomato).
Now that we have completed *rember* try this example: (*rember a lat*) where *a* is sauce and *lat* is (soy sauce and tomato sauce)	(*rember a lat*) is (soy and tomato sauce).

What is (*firsts l*)
where
    l is ((apple peach pumpkin)
       (plum pear cherry)
       (grape raisin pea)
       (bean carrot eggplant))

(apple plum grape bean).

What is (*firsts l*)
where
    l is ((a b) (c d) (e f))

(a c e).

What is (*firsts l*)
where *l* is ()

().

What is (*firsts l*)
where
    l is ((five plums)
      (four)
      (eleven green oranges))

(five four eleven).

What is (*firsts l*)
where
    l is (((five plums) four)
      (eleven green oranges)
      ((no) more))

((five plums) eleven (no)).

In your own words, what does (*firsts l*) do?

We tried the following:
"The function *firsts* takes one argument, a list, which is either a null list or contains only non-empty lists. It builds another list composed of the first S-expression of each internal list."

Cons the Magnificent

See if you can write the function *firsts*
  Remember the Commandments!
	This much is easy:
	
	(**define** *firsts*
	 (**lambda** (*l*)
	  (**cond**
	   ((*null?* *l*) ...)
	   (**else** (*cons* ... (*firsts* (*cdr* *l*)))))))))

Why
 (**define** *firsts*
  (**lambda** (*l*)
   ...))
	Because we always state the function name,
	(**lambda**, and the argument(s) of the
	function.

Why (**cond** ...)	Because we need to ask questions about the actual arguments.
Why ((*null?* *l*) ...)	The First Commandment.
Why (**else**	Because we only have two questions to ask about the list *l*: either it is the null list, or it contains at least one non-empty list.
Why (**else**	See above. And because the last question is always **else**.
Why (*cons*	Because we are building a list—The Second Commandment.
Why (*firsts* (*cdr* *l*))	Because we can only look at one S-expression at a time. To look at the rest, we must recur.
Why)))	Because these are the matching parentheses for (**cond**, (**lambda**, and (**define**, and they always appear at the end of a function definition.

Keeping in mind the definition of (*firsts l*) what is a typical element of the value of (*firsts l*) where *l* is ((a b) (c d) (e f))	a.
What is another typical element?	c, or even e.
Consider the function *seconds* What would be a typical element of the value of (*seconds l*) where *l* is ((a b) (c d) (e f))	b, d, or f.
How do we describe a typical element for (*firsts l*)	As the *car* of an element of *l*—(*car* (*car l*)). See chapter 1.
When we find a typical element of (*firsts l*) what do we do with it?	*cons* it onto the recursion—(*firsts* (*cdr l*)).

The Third Commandment

When building a list, describe the first typical element, and then *cons* it onto the natural recursion.

With The Third Commandment, we can now fill in more of the function *firsts* What does the last line look like now?	(**else** (*cons* (*car* (*car l*)) (*firsts* (*cdr l*)))).
	                    typical natural
	                 element recursion

What does (*firsts* *l*) do

```
(define firsts
  (lambda (l)
    (cond
      ((null? l) ...)
      (else (cons (car (car l))
                  (firsts (cdr l)))))))
```

where *l* is ((a b) (c d) (e f))

Nothing yet. We are still missing one important ingredient in our recipe. The first line ((*null?* *l*) ...) needs a value for the case where *l* is the null list. We can, however, proceed without it for now.

(*null?* *l*) where *l* is ((a b) (c d) (e f))

No, so move to the next line.

What is the meaning of
  (*cons* (*car* (*car* *l*))
    (*firsts* (*cdr* *l*)))

It saves (*car* (*car* *l*)) to *cons* onto (*firsts* (*cdr* *l*)). To find (*firsts* (*cdr* *l*)), we refer to the function with the new argument (*cdr* *l*).

(*null?* *l*) where *l* is ((c d) (e f))

No, so move to the next line.

What is the meaning of
  (*cons* (*car* (*car* *l*))
    (*firsts* (*cdr* *l*)))

Save (*car* (*car* *l*)), and recur with (*firsts* (*cdr* *l*)).

(*null?* *l*) where *l* is ((e f))

No, so move to the next line.

What is the meaning of
  (*cons* (*car* (*car* *l*))
    (*firsts* (*cdr* *l*)))

Save (*car* (*car* *l*)), and recur with (*firsts* (*cdr* *l*)).

(*null?* *l*)

Yes.

Now, what is the value of the line
  ((*null?* *l*) ...)

There is no value; something is missing.

What do we need to *cons* atoms onto?	A list. Remember The Law of Cons.

For the purpose of *cons*ing, what value can we give when (*null? l*) is true?	Since the final value must be a list, we cannot use #t or #f. Let's try (**quote** ()).

With () as a value, we now have three *cons* steps to go back and pick up. We need to:	(a c e).

    I. either
        1. *cons* e onto ()
        2. *cons* c onto the value of 1
        3. *cons* a onto the value of 2

    II. or
        1. *cons* a onto the value of 2
        2. *cons* c onto the value of 3
        3. *cons* e onto ()

    III. or
        cons **a** onto
          the *cons* of c onto
            the *cons* of e onto
              ()

In any case, what is the value of (*firsts l*)

With which of the three alternatives do you feel most comfortable?	Correct! Now you should use that one.

What is (*insertR new old lat*)
where
    new is topping
    old is fudge
and
    lat is (ice cream with fudge for dessert)
	(ice cream with fudge topping for dessert).

(*insertR new old lat*)
where
    new is jalapeño
    old is and
and
    lat is (tacos tamales and salsa)
	(tacos tamales and jalapeño salsa).

(*insertR new old lat*)
where
  new is e
  old is d
and
  lat is (a b c d f g d h)
	(a b c d e f g d h).

In your own words, what does
(*insertR new old lat*) do?
	In our words:
	  "It takes three arguments: the atoms *new*
	  and *old*, and a lat. The function *insertR*
	  builds a lat with *new* inserted to the right
	  of the first occurrence of *old*."

See if you can write the first three lines of
the function *insertR*
	(**define** *insertR*
	  (**lambda** (*new old lat*)
	    (**cond** ...)))

Which argument changes when we recur with *insertR*	*lat*, because we can only look at one of its atoms at a time.

How many questions can we ask about the
lat?
	Two.
	  A lat is either the null list or a non-empty
	  list of atoms.

Which questions do we ask?	First, we ask (*null? lat*). Second, we ask **else**, because **else** is always the last question.

What do we know if (*null? lat*) is not true?	We know that *lat* has at least one element.

Which questions do we ask about the first element?	First, we ask (*eq? (car lat) old*). Then we ask **else**, because there are no other interesting cases.

Now see if you can write the whole function
insertR

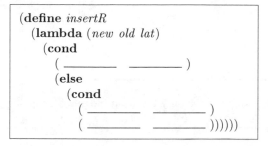

Here is our first attempt.

(**define** *insertR*
· (**lambda** (*new old lat*)
(**cond**
((*null? lat*) (**quote** ()))
(**else**
(**cond**
((*eq? (car lat) old*) (*cdr lat*))
(**else** (*cons (car lat)*
(*insertR new old*
(*cdr lat*)))))))))))

What is the value of the application
(*insertR new old lat*)
that we just determined
where
  new is topping
  old is fudge
and
  lat is (ice cream with fudge for dessert)

(ice cream with for dessert).

So far this is the same as *rember*
What do we do in *insertR* when
(*eq? (car lat) old*) is true?

When (*car lat*) is the same as *old*, we want
to insert *new* to the right.

How is this done?

Let's try *cons*ing *new* onto (*cdr lat*).

Now we have

(**define** *insertR*
(**lambda** (*new old lat*)
(**cond**
((*null? lat*) (**quote** ()))
(**else** (**cond**
((*eq? (car lat) old*)
(*cons new (cdr lat*)))
(**else** (*cons (car lat)*
(*insertR new old*
(*cdr lat*)))))))))

Yes.

So what is (*insertR new old lat*) now where
   new is topping
   old is fudge
and
   lat is (ice cream with fudge for dessert)

(ice cream with topping for dessert).

Is this the list we wanted?

No, we have only replaced fudge with topping.

What still needs to be done?

Somehow we need to include the atom that is the same as *old* before the atom *new*.

How can we include *old* before *new*

Try *consing old* onto (*cons new* (*cdr lat*)).

Now let's write the rest of the function *insertR*

```
(define insertR
  (lambda (new old lat)
    (cond
      ((null? lat) (quote ()))
      (else (cond
              ((eq? (car lat) old)
               (cons old
                 (cons new (cdr lat))))
              (else (cons (car lat)
                      (insertR new old
                        (cdr lat)))))))))
```

When *new* is topping, *old* is fudge, and *lat* is (ice cream with fudge for dessert), the value of the application, (*insertR new old lat*), is
   (ice cream with fudge topping for dessert).
If you got this right, have one.

Now try *insertL*

Hint: *insertL* inserts the atom *new* to the left of the first occurrence of the atom *old* in *lat*

This much is easy, right?

```
(define insertL
  (lambda (new old lat)
    (cond
      ((null? lat) (quote ()))
      (else (cond
              ((eq? (car lat) old)
               (cons new
                 (cons old (cdr lat))))
              (else (cons (car lat)
                      (insertL new old
                        (cdr lat)))))))))
```

Did you think of a different way to do it?

For example,

((*eq?* (*car lat*) *old*)
 (*cons new* (*cons old* (*cdr lat*))))

could have been

((*eq?* (*car lat*) *old*)
 (*cons new lat*))

since (*cons old* (*cdr lat*)) where *old* is *eq?* to (*car lat*) is the same as *lat*.

Now try *subst*

Hint: (*subst new old lat*) replaces the first occurrence of *old* in the *lat* with *new*
For example,
where
   new is topping
   old is fudge
and
   lat is (ice cream with fudge for dessert)
the value is
  (ice cream with topping for dessert)

Now you have the idea.

Obviously,

```
(define subst
  (lambda (new old lat)
    (cond
      ((null? lat) (quote ()))
      (else (cond
              ((eq? (car lat) old)
               (cons new (cdr lat)))
              (else (cons (car lat)
                      (subst new old
                        (cdr lat)))))))))
```

This is the same as one of our incorrect attempts at *insertR*.

Go cons a piece of cake onto your mouth.

Now try *subst2*
  Hint:
    (*subst2 new o1 o2 lat*)
replaces either the first occurrence of *o1* or
the first occurrence of *o2* by *new*
For example,
where
  new is vanilla
  o1 is chocolate
  o2 is banana
and
  lat is (banana ice cream
      with chocolate topping)
the value is
  (vanilla ice cream
   with chocolate topping)

```
(define subst2
  (lambda (new o1 o2 lat)
    (cond
      ((null? lat) (quote ()))
      (else (cond
              ((eq? (car lat) o1)
               (cons new (cdr lat)))
              ((eq? (car lat) o2)
               (cons new (cdr lat)))
              (else (cons (car lat)
                      (subst2 new o1 o2
                        (cdr lat)))))))))
```

Did you think of a better way?

Replace the two *eq?* lines about the (*car lat*)
by
  ((**or** (*eq?* (*car lat*) *o1*) (*eq?* (*car lat*) *o2*))
  (*cons new* (*cdr lat*))).

If you got the last function, go and repeat the cake-consing.

Do you recall what *rember* does?

The function *rember* looks at each atom of a
lat to see if it is the same as the atom *a*. If it
is not, *rember* saves the atom and proceeds.
When it finds the first occurrence of *a*, it
stops and gives the value (*cdr lat*), or the
rest of the lat, so that the value returned is
the original lat, with only that occurrence of
a removed.

Write the function *multirember* which gives as its final value the lat with all occurrences of *a* removed.

```
(define multirember
  (lambda (a lat)
    (cond
      ( _____  _____ )
      (else
        (cond
          ( _____  _____ )
          ( _____  _____ ))))))
```

Hint: What do we want as the value when
    (*eq?* (*car lat*) *a*) is true?
Consider the example
where *a* is cup
and
    lat is (coffee cup tea cup and hick cup)

```
(define multirember
  (lambda (a lat)
    (cond
      ((null? lat) (quote ()))
      (else
        (cond
          ((eq? (car lat) a)
            (multirember a (cdr lat)))
          (else (cons (car lat)
            (multirember a
              (cdr lat)))))))))
```

After the first occurrence of *a*, we now recur with (*multirember a* (*cdr lat*)), in order to remove the other occurrences.

The value of the application is
(coffee tea and hick).

Can you see how *multirember* works?

Possibly not, so we will go through the steps necessary to arrive at the value
    (coffee tea and hick).

(*null? lat*)

No, so move to the next line.

---

else

Yes.

(*eq?* (*car lat*) *a*)

No, so move to the next line.

What is the meaning of
    (*cons* (*car lat*)
      (*multirember a*
        (*cdr lat*)))

Save (*car lat*)—coffee—to be *cons*ed onto the value of (*multirember a* (*cdr lat*)) later. Now determine
    (*multirember a* (*cdr lat*)).

(*null? lat*)

No, so move to the next line.

---

else	Naturally.
(eq? (car lat) a)	Yes, so forget *(car lat)*, and determine *(multirember a (cdr lat))*.
(null? lat)	No, so move to the next line.
else	Yes!
(eq? (car lat) a)	No, so move to the next line.

What is the meaning of
  (cons (car lat)
    (multirember a
      (cdr lat)))
	Save *(car lat)*—**tea**—to be *cons*ed onto the value of *(multirember a (cdr lat))* later. Now determine
	    (multirember a (cdr lat)).

(null? lat)	No, so move to the next line.
else	Okay, move on.
(eq? (car lat) a)	Yes, so forget *(car lat)*, and determine *(multirember a (cdr lat))*.
(null? lat)	No, so move to the next line.
(eq? (car lat) a)	No, so move to the next line.

What is the meaning of
  (cons (car lat)
    (multirember a
      (cdr lat)))
	Save *(car lat)*—**and**—to be *cons*ed onto the value of *(multirember a (cdr lat))* later. Now determine
	    (multirember a (cdr lat)).

(*null? lat*)	No, so move to the next line.
(*eq?* (*car lat*) *a*)	No, so move to the next line.

What is the meaning of
   (*cons* (*car lat*)
    (*multirember a*
     (*cdr lat*)))
	Save (*car lat*)—hick—to be *cons*ed onto the value of (*multirember a* (*cdr lat*)) later. Now determine
	   (*multirember a* (*cdr lat*)).

(*null? lat*)	No, so move to the next line.
(*eq?* (*car lat*) *a*)	Yes, so forget (*car lat*), and determine (*multirember a* (*cdr lat*)).
(*null? lat*)	Yes, so the value is ().
Are we finished?	No, we still have several *cons*es to pick up.
What do we do next?	We *cons* the most recent (*car lat*) we have—hick—onto ().
What do we do next?	We *cons* and onto (hick).
What do we do next?	We *cons* tea onto (and hick).
What do we do next?	We *cons* coffee onto (tea and hick).
Are we finished now?	Yes.

Now write the function *multiinsertR*

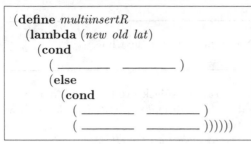

```
(define multiinsertR
  (lambda (new old lat)
    (cond
      ( _____  _____ )
      (else
        (cond
          ( _____  _____ )
          ( _____  _____ ))))))
```

```
(define multiinsertR
  (lambda (new old lat)
    (cond
      ((null? lat) (quote ()))
      (else
        (cond
          ((eq? (car lat) old)
           (cons (car lat)
             (cons new
               (multiinsertR new old
                 (cdr lat)))))
          (else (cons (car lat)
                  (multiinsertR new old
                    (cdr lat)))))))))
```

It would also be correct to use *old* in place of (*car lat*) because we know that (*eq?* (*car lat*) *old*).

Is this function defined correctly?

```
(define multiinsertL
  (lambda (new old lat)
    (cond
      ((null? lat) (quote ()))
      (else
        (cond
          ((eq? (car lat) old)
           (cons new
             (cons old
               (multiinsertL new old
                 lat))))
          (else (cons (car lat)
                  (multiinsertL new old
                    (cdr lat)))))))))
```

Not quite. To find out why, go through
(*multiinsertL new old lat*)
where
  new is fried
  old is fish
and
  lat is (chips and fish or fish and fried).

Was the terminal condition ever reached?

No, because we never get past the first occurrence of *old*.

Now, try to write the function *multiinsertL* again:

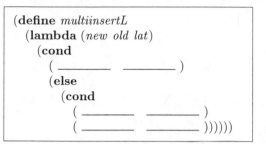

```
(define multiinsertL
  (lambda (new old lat)
    (cond
      ( _____  _____ )
      (else
        (cond
          ( _____  _____ )
          ( _____  _____ )))))))
```

```
(define multiinsertL
  (lambda (new old lat)
    (cond
      ((null? lat) (quote ()))
      (else
        (cond
          ((eq? (car lat) old)
           (cons new
             (cons old
               (multiinsertL new old
                 (cdr lat)))))
          (else (cons (car lat)
                  (multiinsertL new old
                    (cdr lat)))))))))))
```

The Fourth Commandment

(preliminary)

Always change at least one argument while recurring. It must be changed to be closer to termination. The changing argument must be tested in the termination condition: when using *cdr*, test termination with *null?*.

Now write the function *multisubst*

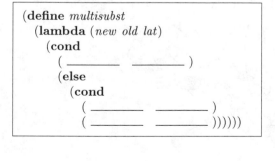

```
(define multisubst
  (lambda (new old lat)
    (cond
      ( _____  _____ )
      (else
        (cond
          ( _____  _____ )
          ( _____  _____ )))))))
```

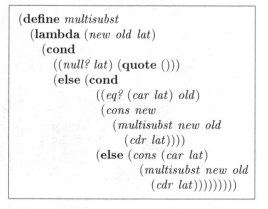

```
(define multisubst
  (lambda (new old lat)
    (cond
      ((null? lat) (quote ()))
      (else (cond
              ((eq? (car lat) old)
               (cons new
                 (multisubst new old
                   (cdr lat))))
              (else (cons (car lat)
                      (multisubst new old
                        (cdr lat)))))))))
```

Is 14 an atom?	Yes, because all numbers are atoms.

Is (*atom?* n) true or false where n is 14	True, because 14 is an atom.

Is −3 a number?	Yes, but we do not consider negative numbers.

Is 3.14159 a number?	Yes, but we consider only whole numbers.

Are −3 and 3.14159 numbers?	Yes, but the only numbers we use are the nonnegative integers (i.e., 0, 1, 2, 3, 4, ...).

What is (*add1*[1] n) where n is 67	68.

---
[1] L: 1+
```
S: (define add1
      (lambda (n)
        (+ n 1))))
```

What is (*add1* 67)	Also 68,
	   because we don't need to say "where n is
	   67" when the argument is a number.

What is (*sub1*[1] n) where n is 5	4.

---
[1] L: 1-
```
S: (define sub1
      (lambda (n)
        (- n 1))))
```

What is (*sub1* 0)

No answer.[1]

[1] (*sub1 n*), where *n* is 0, has no answer because we consider only nonnegative numbers. In practice, this result is -1.

Is (*zero?*[1] 0) true or false?

True.

[1] L: `zerop`

Is (*zero?* 1492) true or false?

False.

What is (✢ 46 12)

58.

Try to write the function ✢
    Hint: It uses *zero?* *add1*[1] and *sub1*[1]

```
(define ✢ [1]
  (lambda (n m)
    (cond
      ((zero? m) n)
      (else (add1 (✢ n (sub1 m)))))))
```

Wasn't that easy?

[1] Remember to use our definitions for `add1` and `sub1`.

[1] L, S: This is like +. Write it as `o+` (see preface).

But didn't we just violate The First Commandment?

Yes, but we can treat *zero?* like *null?* since *zero?* asks if a number is empty and *null?* asks if a list is empty.

If *zero?* is like *null?*
is *add1* like *cons*

Yes! *cons* builds lists and *add1* builds numbers.

What is (− 14 3)	11.

What is (− 17 9)	8.

What is (− 18 25)	No answer. There are no negative numbers.

Try to write the function − Hint: Use *sub1*	How about this:

```
(define −  1
  (lambda (n m)
    (cond
      ((zero? m) n)
      (else (sub1 (− n (sub1 m)))))))
```

------
[1] L, S: This is like -. Write it as o- (see preface).

Can you describe how (− *n* *m*) works?	It takes two numbers as arguments, and reduces the second until it hits zero. It subtracts one from the result as many times as it did to cause the second one to reach zero.

Is this a tup? (2 11 3 79 47 6)	Yes: tup is short for tuple.

Is this a tup? (8 55 5 555)	Yes, of course, it is also a list of numbers.

Is this a tup? (1 2 8 apple 4 3)	No, it is just a list of atoms.

Is this a tup? (3 (7 4) 13 9)	No, because it is not a list of numbers. (7 4) is not a number.

Is this a tup? ()	Yes, it is a list of zero numbers. This special case is the empty tup.
What is (*addtup tup*) where *tup* is (3 5 2 8)	18.
What is (*addtup tup*) where *tup* is (15 6 7 12 3)	43.
What does *addtup* do?	It builds a number by totaling all the numbers in its argument.
What is the natural way to build numbers from a list?	Use ✢ in place of *cons*: ✢ builds numbers in the same way as *cons* builds lists.
When building lists with *cons* the value of the terminal condition is () What should be the value of the terminal condition when building numbers with ✢	0.
What is the natural terminal condition for a list?	(*null? l*).
What is the natural terminal condition for a tup?	(*null? tup*).
When we build a number from a list of numbers, what should the terminal condition line look like?	((*null? tup*) 0), just as ((*null? l*) (**quote** ())) is often the terminal condition line for lists.
What is the terminal condition line of *addtup*	((*null? tup*) 0).

How is a lat defined?	It is either an empty list, or it contains an atom, (*car lat*), and a rest, (*cdr lat*), that is also a lat.
How is a tup defined?	It is either an empty list, or it contains a number and a rest that is also a tup.
What is used in the natural recursion on a list?	(*cdr lat*).
What is used in the natural recursion on a tup?	(*cdr tup*).
Why?	Because the rest of a non-empty list is a list and the rest of a non-empty tup is a tup.
How many questions do we need to ask about a list?	Two.
How many questions do we need to ask about a tup?	Two, because it is either empty or it is a number and a rest, which is again a tup.
How is a number defined?	It is either zero or it is one added to a rest, where rest is again a number.
What is the natural terminal condition for numbers?	(*zero? n*).
What is the natural recursion on a number?	(*sub1 n*).
How many questions do we need to ask about a number?	Two.

What does *cons* do?	It builds lists.
What does *addtup* do?	It builds a number by totaling all the numbers in a tup.
What is the terminal condition line of *addtup*	((*null? tup*) 0).
What is the natural recursion for *addtup*	(*addtup* (*cdr tup*)).
What does *addtup* use to build a number?	It uses ✢, because ✢ builds numbers, too!

Fill in the dots in the following definition:
 	
(**define** *addtup*
  (**lambda** (*tup*)
    (**cond**
      ((*null? tup*) 0)
      (**else** ...))))
	Here is what we filled in:
	  (✢ (*car tup*) (*addtup* (*cdr tup*))).
	Notice the similarity between this line, and the last line of the function *rember*:
	  (*cons* (*car lat*) (*rember a* (*cdr lat*))).

What is (× 5 3)	15.
What is (× 13 4)	52.

What does $(\times\ n\ m)$ do?	It builds up a number by adding n up m times.

What is the terminal condition line for $\times$	$((zero?\ m)\ 0)$, because $n \times 0 = 0$.

Since $(zero?\ m)$ is the terminal condition, m must eventually be reduced to zero. What function is used to do this?	$sub1$.

The Fourth Commandment

(first revision)

Always change at least one argument while recurring. It must be changed to be closer to termination. The changing argument must be tested in the termination condition:

when using *cdr*, test termination with *null?* and
when using *sub1*, test termination with *zero?*.

What is another name for $(\times\ n\ (sub1\ m))$ in this case?	It's the natural recursion for $\times$.

Try to write the function $\times$	```(define ×¹```

```
(define ×[1]
  (lambda (n m)
    (cond
      ((zero? m) 0)
      (else (✢ n (× n (sub1 m)))))))
```

---

[1] L, S: This is like *.

What is (× 12 3)	36,
	    but let's follow through the function one
	    time to see how we get this value.

(*zero?* *m*)	No.

What is the meaning of
  (✦ *n* (× *n* (*sub1* *m*)))
	It adds *n* (where *n* = 12) to the natural
	recursion. If × is correct then
	  (× 12 (*sub1* 3))
	should be 24.

What are the new arguments of (× *n* *m*)	*n* is 12, and *m* is 2.
(*zero?* *m*)	No.
What is the meaning of (✦ *n* (× *n* (*sub1* *m*)))	It adds *n* (where *n* = 12) to (× *n* (*sub1* *m*)).
What are the new arguments of (× *n* *m*)	*n* is 12, and *m* is 1.
(*zero?* *m*)	No.
What is the meaning of (✦ *n* (× *n* (*sub1* *m*)))	It adds *n* (where *n* = 12) to (× *n* (*sub1* *m*)).
What is the value of the line ((*zero?* *m*) 0)	0, because (*zero?* *m*) is now true.
Are we finished yet?	No.

Why not?	Because we still have three ✢es to pick up.

What is the value of the original application?	Add 12 to 12 to 12 to 0 yielding **36**, Notice that n has been ✢ed m times.

Argue, using equations, that × is the conventional multiplication of nonnegative integers, where n is 12 and m is 3.	$\begin{aligned} (\times\ 12\ 3) \quad &= \quad 12\ +\ (\times\ 12\ 2) \\ &= \quad 12\ +\ 12\ +\ (\times\ 12\ 1) \\ &= \quad 12\ +\ 12\ +\ 12\ +\ (\times\ 12\ 0) \\ &= \quad 12\ +\ 12\ +\ 12\ +\ 0, \end{aligned}$ which is as we expected. This technique works for all recursive functions, not just those that use numbers. You can use this approach to write functions as well as to argue their correctness.

Again, why is 0 the value for the terminal condition line in ×	Because 0 will not affect +. That is, $n + 0 = n.$

The Fifth Commandment

When building a value with ✢ , always use 0 for the value of the terminating line, for adding 0 does not change the value of an addition.

When building a value with ×, always use 1 for the value of the terminating line, for multiplying by 1 does not change the value of a multiplication.

When building a value with *cons***, always consider () for the value of the terminating line.**

What is $(tup+\ tup1\ tup2)$
where
   $tup1$ is (3 6 9 11 4)
and
   $tup2$ is (8 5 2 0 7)
	(11 11 11 11 11).

What is (*tup+* *tup1* *tup2*)
 where
   tup1 is (2 3)
 and
   tup2 is (4 6)
	(6 9).

What does (*tup+* *tup1* *tup2*) do?	It adds the first number of *tup1* to the first number of *tup2*, then it adds the second number of *tup1* to the second number of *tup2*, and so on, building a tup of the answers, for tups of the same length.

What is unusual about *tup+*	It looks at each element of two tups at the same time, or in other words, it recurs on two tups.

If you recur on one tup how many questions do you have to ask?	Two, they are (*null? tup*) and **else**.

When recurring on two tups, how many questions need to be asked about the tups?	Four: if the first tup is empty or non-empty, and if the second tup is empty or non-empty.

Do you mean the questions
   (**and** (*null? tup1*) (*null? tup2*))
   (*null? tup1*)
   (*null? tup2*)
 and
   else
	Yes.

Can the first *tup* be () at the same time as the second is other than ()	No, because the tups must have the same length.

Does this mean
   (**and** (*null? tup1*) (*null? tup2*))
 and
   else
 are the only questions we need to ask?
	Yes,
	   because (*null? tup1*) is true exactly when (*null? tup2*) is true.

Write the function *tup+*	```
	(define tup+
	  (lambda (tup1 tup2)
	    (cond
	      ((and (null? tup1) (null? tup2))
	       (quote ()))
	      (else
	        (cons (⊹ (car tup1) (car tup2))
	          (tup+
	            (cdr tup1) (cdr tup2)))))))
	``

What are the arguments of ⊹ in the last line?	(*car tup1*) and (*car tup2*).
What are the arguments of *cons* in the last line?	(⊹ (*car tup1*) (*car tup2*)) and (*tup+* (*cdr tup1*) (*cdr tup2*)).

What is (*tup+ tup1 tup2*)
where
  tup1 is (3 7)
and
  tup2 is (4 6)
	(7 13).
	But let's see how it works.

(*null? tup1*)	No.

(*cons*
  (⊹ (*car tup1*) (*car tup2*))
  (*tup+* (*cdr tup1*) (*cdr tup2*)))
	cons 7 onto the natural recursion:
	  (*tup+* (*cdr tup1*) (*cdr tup2*)).

Why does the natural recursion include the *cdr* of both arguments?	Because the typical element of the final value uses the *car* of both tups, so now we are ready to consider the rest of both tups.

(*null? tup1*)
where
  tup1 is now (7)
and
  tup2 is now (6)
	No.

(*cons*
  (✢ (*car tup1*) (*car tup2*))
  (*tup+* (*cdr tup1*) (*cdr tup2*)))
	cons 13 onto the natural recursion.

(*null? tup1*)	Yes.

Then, what must be the value?	(), because (*null? tup2*) must be true.

What is the value of the application?	(7 13). That is, the *cons* of 7 onto the *cons* of 13 onto ().

What problem arises when we want
(*tup+ tup1 tup2*)
where
  tup1 is (3 7)
and
  tup2 is (4 6 8 1)
	No answer, since *tup1* will become null before *tup2*.
	  See The First Commandment: We did not ask all the necessary questions!
	But, we would like the final value to be
	  (7 13 8 1).

Can we still write *tup+* even if the tups are not the same length? ·	Yes!

What new terminal condition line can we add to get the correct final value?	Add ((*null? tup1*) *tup2*).

What is (*tup+ tup1 tup2*)
where
  tup1 is (3 7 8 1)
and
  tup2 is (4 6)
	No answer, since *tup2* will become null before *tup1*.
	  See The First Commandment: We did not ask all the necessary questions!

What do we need to include in our function?	We need to ask two more questions: (*null? tup1*) and (*null? tup2*).

What does the second new line look like?	((*null? tup2*) *tup1*).

Here is a definition of *tup+* that works for any two tups:

```
(define tup+
  (lambda (tup1 tup2)
    (cond
      ((and (null? tup1) (null? tup2))
       (quote ()))
      ((null? tup1) tup2)
      ((null? tup2) tup1)
      (else
        (cons (+ (car tup1) (car tup2))
          (tup+
            (cdr tup1) (cdr tup2)))))))
```

Can you simplify it?

```
(define tup+
  (lambda (tup1 tup2)
    (cond
      ((null? tup1) tup2)
      ((null? tup2) tup1)
      (else
        (cons (+ (car tup1) (car tup2))
          (tup+
            (cdr tup1) (cdr tup2)))))))
```

Does the order of the two terminal conditions matter?	No.

Is **else** the last question?	Yes, because either (*null? tup1*) or (*null? tup2*) is true if either one of them does not contain at least one number.

What is (> 12 133)	#f—false.

What is (> 120 11)	#t —true.

On how many numbers do we have to recur?	Two, *n* and *m*.

How do we recur?	With (*sub1 n*) and (*sub1 m*).

When do we recur?	When we know neither number is equal to 0.

How many questions do we have to ask about *n* and *m*	Three: (*zero? n*), (*zero? m*), and **else**.

Can you write the function > now using *zero?* and *sub1*	How about

```
(define >
  (lambda (n m)
    (cond
      ((zero? m) #t)
      ((zero? n) #f)
      (else (> (sub1 n) (sub1 m)))))))
```

Is the way we wrote (> *n m*) correct?	No, try it for the case where *n* and *m* are the same number. Let *n* and *m* be **3**.
(*zero?* **3**)	No, so move to the next question.
(*zero?* **3**)	No, so move to the next question.
What is the meaning of (> (*sub1 n*) (*sub1 m*))	Recur, but with both arguments reduced by one.
(*zero?* **2**)	No, so move to the next question.
(*zero?* **2**)	No, so move to the next question.
What is the meaning of (> (*sub1 n*) (*sub1 m*))	Recur, but with both arguments closer to zero by one.
(*zero?* **1**)	No, so move to the next question.
(*zero?* **1**)	No, so move to the next question.
What is the meaning of (> (*sub1 n*) (*sub1 m*))	Recur, but with both arguments reduced by one.

(*zero?* 0)	Yes, so the value of (> *n* *m*) is #t.
Is this correct?	No, because 3 is **not** greater than 3.
Does the order of the two terminal conditions matter?	Think about it.
Does the order of the two terminal conditions matter?	Try it out!
Does the order of the two previous answers matter?	Yes. Think first, then try.

How can we change the function > to take care of this subtle problem?

Switch the *zero?* lines:

```
(define >
  (lambda (n m)
    (cond
      ((zero? n) #f)
      ((zero? m) #t)
      (else (> (sub1 n) (sub1 m)))))))
```

What is (< 4 6)	#t.
(< 8 3)	#f.
(< 6 6)	#f.

Now try to write <

```
(define <
  (lambda (n m)
    (cond
      ((zero? m) #f)
      ((zero? n) #t)
      (else (< (sub1 n) (sub1 m)))))))
```

Here is the definition of =

```
(define =
  (lambda (n m)
    (cond
      ((zero? m) (zero? n))
      ((zero? n) #f)
      (else (= (sub1 n) (sub1 m))))))
```

```
(define =
  (lambda (n m)
    (cond
      ((> n m) #f)
      ((< n m) #f)
      (else #t))))
```

Rewrite = using < and >

Does this mean we have two different functions for testing equality of atoms?

Yes, they are = for atoms that are numbers and *eq?* for the others.

(↑ 1 1)

1.

(↑ 2 3)

8.

(↑ 5 3)

125.

Now write the function ↑
  Hint: See the The First and Fifth Commandments.

```
(define ↑¹
  (lambda (n m)
    (cond
      ((zero? m) 1)
      (else (× n (↑ n (sub1 m)))))))
```

---

[1] L, S: This is like **expt**.

What is a good name for this function?

```
(define ???
  (lambda (n m)
    (cond
      ((< n m) 0)
      (else (add1 (??? (− n m) m))))))
```

We have never seen this kind of definition before; the natural recursion also looks strange.

What does the first question check?	It determines whether the first argument is less than the second one.

And what happens in the second line?	We recur with a first argument from which we subtract the second argument. When the function returns, we add 1 to the result.

So what does the function do?	It counts how many times the second argument fits into the first one.

And what do we call this?	Division.

$$\begin{array}{l}
(\textbf{define} \div^1 \\
\quad (\textbf{lambda} \ (n \ m) \\
\quad\quad (\textbf{cond} \\
\quad\quad\quad ((< n \ m) \ 0) \\
\quad\quad\quad (\textbf{else} \ (add1 \ (\div \ (- \ n \ m) \ m)))))))
\end{array}$$

---

[1] L: (defun quotient (n m)
        (values (truncate (/ n m))))
   S: This is like quotient.

What is $(\div \ 15 \ 4)$	Easy, it is 3.

How do we get there?	Easy, too:

$$\begin{aligned}
(\div \ 15 \ 4) \ &= \ 1 \ + \ (\div \ 11 \ 4) \\
&= \ 1 \ + \ (1 \ + \ (\div \ 7 \ 4)) \\
&= \ 1 \ + \ (1 \ + \ (1 \ + \ (\div \ 3 \ 4))) \\
&= \ 1 \ + \ (1 \ + \ (1 \ + \ 0)).
\end{aligned}$$

Wouldn't a (ham and cheese on rye) be good right now?

Don't forget the mustard!

What is the value of (*length lat*)
where
   lat is (hotdogs with mustard sauerkraut
         and pickles)

6.

What is (*length lat*)
where
   lat is (ham and cheese on rye)

5.

Now try to write the function *length*

```
(define length
  (lambda (lat)
    (cond
      ((null? lat) 0)
      (else (add1 (length (cdr lat)))))))
```

What is (*pick n lat*)
where *n* is 4
and
   lat is (lasagna spaghetti ravioli
        macaroni meatball)

macaroni.

What is (*pick* 0 *lat*)
where *lat* is (a)

No answer.

Try to write the function *pick*

```
(define pick
  (lambda (n lat)
    (cond
      ((zero? (sub1 n)) (car lat))
      (else (pick (sub1 n) (cdr lat))))))
```

What is (*rempick n lat*)
where *n* is 3
and
   lat is (hotdogs with hot mustard)

(hotdogs with mustard).

Now try to write *rempick*

```
(define rempick
  (lambda (n lat)
    (cond
      ((zero? (sub1 n)) (cdr lat))
      (else (cons (car lat)
                  (rempick (sub1 n)
                           (cdr lat)))))))
```

Is (*number?*[1] *a*) true or false
where *a* is tomato

False.

---

[1] L: numberp

Is (*number?* 76) true or false?

True.

Can you write *number?* which is true if its
argument is a numeric atom and false if it is
anthing else?

No: *number?*, like *add1*, *sub1*, *zero?*, *car*,
cdr, *cons*, *null?*, *eq?*, and *atom?*, is a
primitive function.

Now using *number?* write the function
no-nums which gives as a final value a lat
obtained by removing all the numbers from
the lat. For example,
where
    lat is (5 pears 6 prunes 9 dates)
the value of (*no-nums lat*) is
    (pears prunes dates)

```
(define no-nums
  (lambda (lat)
    (cond
      ((null? lat) (quote ()))
      (else (cond
              ((number? (car lat))
               (no-nums (cdr lat)))
              (else (cons (car lat)
                          (no-nums
                            (cdr lat)))))))))
```

Now write *all-nums* which extracts a tup from a lat using all the numbers in the lat.

```
(define all-nums
  (lambda (lat)
    (cond
      ((null? lat) (quote ()))
      (else
        (cond
          ((number? (car lat))
           (cons (car lat)
             (all-nums (cdr lat))))
          (else (all-nums (cdr lat))))))))
```

Write the function *eqan?* which is true if its two arguments (*a1* and *a2*) are the same atom. Remember to use = for numbers and *eq?* for all other atoms.

```
(define eqan?
  (lambda (a1 a2)
    (cond
      ((and (number? a1) (number? a2))
       (= a1 a2))
      ((or (number? a1) (number? a2))
       #f)
      (else (eq? a1 a2)))))
```

Can we assume that all functions written using *eq?* can be generalized by replacing *eq?* by *eqan?*

Yes, except, of course, for *eqan?* itself.

Now write the function *occur* which counts the number of times an atom *a* appears in a *lat*

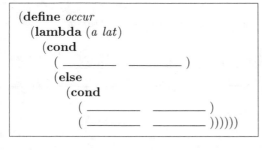

```
(define occur
  (lambda (a lat)
    (cond
      ( _____  _____ )
      (else
        (cond
          ( _____  _____ )
          ( _____  _____ ))))))
```

```
(define occur
  (lambda (a lat)
    (cond
      ((null? lat) 0)
      (else
        (cond
          ((eq? (car lat) a)
           (add1 (occur a (cdr lat))))
          (else (occur a (cdr lat))))))))
```

5.
"Oh My Gawd": It's Full of Stars

Write the function *one?* where (*one? n*) is #t
if *n* is 1 and #f (i.e., false) otherwise.

```
(define one?
  (lambda (n)
    (cond
      ((zero? n) #f)
      (else (zero? (sub1 n))))))
```

or

```
(define one?
  (lambda (n)
    (cond
      (else (= n 1)))))
```

Guess how we can further simplify this
function, making it a one-liner.

By removing the (**cond** ...) clause:

```
(define one?
  (lambda (n)
    (= n 1)))
```

Now rewrite the function *rempick* that
removes the nth atom from a lat. For
example,
where
  n is 3
and
  lat is (lemon meringue salty pie)
the value of (*rempick n lat*) is
  (lemon meringue pie)
Use the function *one?* in your answer.

```
(define rempick
  (lambda (n lat)
    (cond
      ((one? n) (cdr lat))
      (else (cons (car lat)
                  (rempick (sub1 n)
                           (cdr lat)))))))
```

What is (*rember* a l*)
where *a* is cup
and
    l is ((coffee) cup ((tea) cup)
       (and (hick)) cup)
"*rember**" is pronounced "rember-star."

((coffee) ((tea)) (and (hick))).

What is (*rember* a l*)
where *a* is sauce
and
    l is (((tomato sauce))
       ((bean) sauce)
       (and ((flying)) sauce))

(((tomato))
 ((bean))
 (and ((flying)))).

Now write *rember**[†]
Here is the skeleton:

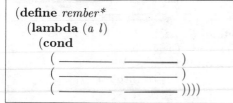

```
(define rember*
  (lambda (a l)
    (cond
      (_____  _____ )
      (_____  _____ )
      (_____  _____ )))))
```

```
(define rember*
  (lambda (a l)
    (cond
      ((null? l) (quote ()))
      ((atom? (car l))
       (cond
         ((eq? (car l) a)
          (rember* a (cdr l)))
         (else (cons (car l)
                (rember* a (cdr l))))))
      (else (cons (rember* a (car l))
             (rember* a (cdr l))))))))
```

Using arguments from one of our previous
examples, follow through this to see how it
works. Notice that now we are recurring
down the *car* of the list, instead of just the
cdr of the list.

[†] " ...* " makes us think "oh my gawd."

(*lat? l*)
where
    l is (((tomato sauce))
       ((bean) sauce)
       (and ((flying)) sauce))

#f.

Is (*car l*) an atom
where
  l is (((tomato sauce))
     ((bean) sauce)
     (and ((flying)) sauce))

No.

What is (*insertR* new old l*)
where
  new is roast
  old is chuck
and
  l is ((how much (wood))
     could
     ((a (wood) chuck))
     (((chuck)))
     (if (a) ((wood chuck)))
     could chuck wood)

((how much (wood))
could
((a (wood) chuck roast))
(((chuck roast)))
(if (a) ((wood chuck roast)))
could chuck roast wood).

Now write the function *insertR** which
inserts the atom *new* to the right of *old*
regardless of where *old* occurs.

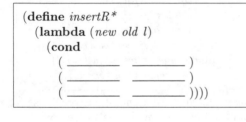

```
(define insertR*
  (lambda (new old l)
    (cond
      ( _____  _____ )
      ( _____  _____ )
      ( _____  _____ ))))
```

```
(define insertR*
  (lambda (new old l)
    (cond
      ((null? l) (quote ()))
      ((atom? (car l))
       (cond
         ((eq? (car l) old)
          (cons old
            (cons new
              (insertR* new old
                (cdr l)))))
         (else (cons (car l)
                 (insertR* new old
                   (cdr l))))))
      (else (cons (insertR* new old
                    (car l))
              (insertR* new old
                (cdr l)))))))
```

How are *insertR** and *rember** similar?

Each function asks three questions.

The First Commandment

(final version)

When recurring on a list of atoms, *lat*, ask two questions about it: (*null? lat*) and else.

When recurring on a number, *n*, ask two questions about it: (*zero? n*) and else.

When recurring on a list of S-expressions, *l*, ask three question about it: (*null? l*), (*atom? (car l)*), and else.

How are *insertR** and *rember** similar?	Each function recurs on the *car* of its argument when it finds out that the argument's *car* is a list.
How are *rember** and *multirember* different?	The function *multirember* does not recur with the *car*. The function *rember** recurs with the *car* as well as with the *cdr*. It recurs with the *car* when it finds out that the *car* is a list.
How are *insertR** and *rember** similar?	They both recur with the *car*, whenever the *car* is a list, as well as with the *cdr*.
How are all *-functions similar?	They all ask three questions and recur with the *car* as well as with the *cdr*, whenever the *car* is a list.
Why?	Because all *-functions work on lists that are either — empty, — an atom *cons*ed onto a list, or — a list *cons*ed onto a list.

(*occursomething a l*)   5.
where
   a is banana
and
  l is ((banana)
     (split ((((banana ice)))
         (cream (banana))
         sherbet))
     (banana)
     (bread)
     (banana brandy))

What is a better name for   *occur**.
  occursomething

Write *occur**

```
(define occur*
  (lambda (a l)
    (cond
      (_____ _____ )
      (_____ _____ )
      (_____ _____ ))))
```

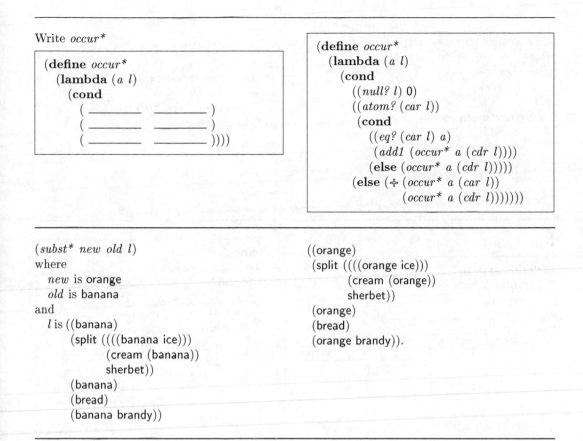

```
(define occur*
  (lambda (a l)
    (cond
      ((null? l) 0)
      ((atom? (car l))
       (cond
         ((eq? (car l) a)
          (add1 (occur* a (cdr l))))
         (else (occur* a (cdr l)))))
      (else (+ (occur* a (car l))
               (occur* a (cdr l)))))))
```

(*subst** *new old l*)
where
  new is orange
  old is banana
and
  l is ((banana)
         (split ((((banana ice)))
                (cream (banana))
                sherbet))
         (banana)
         (bread)
         (banana brandy))

((orange)
 (split ((((orange ice)))
        (cream (orange))
        sherbet))
 (orange)
 (bread)
 (orange brandy)).

Write *subst**

```
(define subst*
  (lambda (new old l)
    (cond
      (_____ _____ )
      (_____ _____ )
      (_____ _____ ))))
```

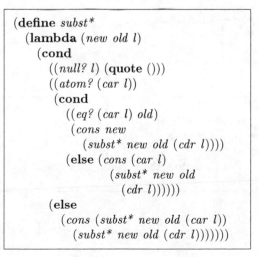

```
(define subst*
  (lambda (new old l)
    (cond
      ((null? l) (quote ()))
      ((atom? (car l))
       (cond
         ((eq? (car l) old)
          (cons new
                (subst* new old (cdr l))))
         (else (cons (car l)
                     (subst* new old
                             (cdr l))))))
      (else
       (cons (subst* new old (car l))
             (subst* new old (cdr l)))))))
```

What is (*insertL* new old l*)
where
  new is pecker
  old is chuck
and
  l is ((how much (wood))
      could
      ((a (wood) chuck))
      (((chuck)))
      (if (a) ((wood chuck)))
      could chuck wood)

((how much (wood))
could
((a (wood) pecker chuck))
(((pecker chuck)))
(if (a) ((wood pecker chuck)))
could pecker chuck wood).

Write *insertL**

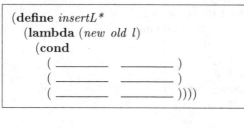

```
(define insertL*
  (lambda (new old l)
    (cond
      ( _____  _____ )
      ( _____  _____ )
      ( _____  _____ )))))
```

```
(define insertL*
  (lambda (new old l)
    (cond
      ((null? l) (quote ()))
      ((atom? (car l))
       (cond
         ((eq? (car l) old)
          (cons new
            (cons old
              (insertL* new old
                (cdr l)))))
         (else (cons (car l)
                 (insertL* new old
                   (cdr l))))))
      (else (cons (insertL* new old
                    (car l))
              (insertL* new old
                (cdr l)))))))))
```

(*member* a l*)
where *a* is chips
and
  l is ((potato) (chips ((with) fish) (chips)))

#t, because the atom chips appears in the
list *l*.

Write *member*

```
(define member*
  (lambda (a l)
    (cond
      ( _____  _____ )
      ( _____  _____ )
      ( _____  _____ ))))
```

```
(define member*
  (lambda (a l)
    (cond
      ((null? l) #f)
      ((atom? (car l))
       (or (eq? (car l) a)
           (member* a (cdr l))))
      (else (or (member* a (car l))
                (member* a (cdr l))))))))
```

What is (*member* a l*)
where
  a is chips
and
  l is ((potato) (chips ((with) fish) (chips)))
	#t.

Which chips did it find?	((potato) (<u>chips</u> ((with) fish) (chips))).
What is (*leftmost l*) where *l* is ((potato) (chips ((with) fish) (chips)))	potato.
What is (*leftmost l*) where *l* is (((hot) (tuna (and))) cheese)	hot.
What is (*leftmost l*) where *l* is (((() four)) 17 (seventeen))	No answer.
What is (*leftmost* (**quote** ()))	No answer.
Can you describe what *leftmost* does?	Here is our description: "The function *leftmost* finds the leftmost atom in a non-empty list of S-expressions that does not contain the empty list."

Is *leftmost* a *-function?	It works on lists of S-expressions, but it only recurs on the *car*.

Does *leftmost* need to ask questions about all three possible cases?	No, it only needs to ask two questions. We agreed that *leftmost* works on non-empty lists that don't contain empty lists.

Now see if you can write the function
leftmost

```
(define leftmost
  (lambda (l)
    (cond
      ( _____  _____ )
      ( _____  _____ ))))
```

```
(define leftmost
  (lambda (l)
    (cond
      ((atom? (car l)) (car l))
      (else (leftmost (car l))))))
```

Do you remember what (**or** ...) does?	(**or** ...) asks questions one at a time until it finds one that is true. Then (**or** ...) stops, making its value true. If it cannot find a true argument, the value of (**or** ...) is false.

What is
   (**and** (*atom?* (*car l*))
     (*eq?* (*car l*) *x*))
where
  x is pizza
and
  l is (mozzarella pizza)

#f.

Why is it false?	Since (**and** ...) asks (*atom?* (*car l*)), which is true, it then asks (*eq?* (*car l*) *x*), which is false; hence it is #f.

Chapter 5

What is
  (**and** (*atom?* (*car l*))
    (*eq?* (*car l*) *x*))
where
  x is pizza
and
  l is ((mozzarella mushroom) pizza)

#f.

Why is it false?

Since (**and** ...) asks (*atom?* (*car l*)), and (*car l*) is not an atom; so it is #f.

Give an example for *x* and *l* where
  (**and** (*atom?* (*car l*))
    (*eq?* (*car l*) *x*))
is true.

Here's one:
  x is pizza
and
  l is (pizza (tastes good)).

Put in your own words what (**and** ...) does.

We put it in our words:
  "(**and** ...) asks questions one at a time
  until it finds one whose value is false. Then
  (**and** ...) stops with false. If none of the
  expressions are false, (**and** ...) is true."

True or false: it is possible that one of the arguments of (**and** ...) and (**or** ...) is not considered?[1]

True, because (**and** ...) stops if the first argument has the value #f, and (**or** ...) stops if the first argument has the value #t.

---

[1] (**cond** ...) also has the property of not considering all of its arguments. Because of this property, however, neither (**and** ...) nor (**or** ...) can be **defined** as functions in terms of (**cond** ...), though both (**and** ...) and (**or** ...) can be expressed as abbreviations of (**cond** ...)-expressions:
  (**and** α β) = (**cond** (α β) (**else** #f))
and
  (**or** α β) = (**cond** (α #t) (**else** β))

(*eqlist?* *l1* *l2*)
where
  l1 is (strawberry ice cream)
and
  l2 is (strawberry ice cream)

#t.

(*eqlist?* l1 l2)
 where
    l1 is (strawberry ice cream)
 and
    l2 is (strawberry cream ice)
	#f.

(*eqlist?* l1 l2)
 where
    l1 is (banana ((split)))
 and
    l2 is ((banana) (split))
	#f.

(*eqlist?* l1 l2)
 where
    l1 is (beef ((sausage)) (and (soda)))
 and
    l2 is (beef ((salami)) (and (soda)))
	#f, but almost #t.

(*eqlist?* l1 l2)
 where
    l1 is (beef ((sausage)) (and (soda)))
 and
    l2 is (beef ((sausage)) (and (soda)))
	#t. That's better.

What is *eqlist?*	It is a function that determines if two lists are equal.

How many questions will *eqlist?* have to ask about its arguments?	Nine.

Can you explain why there are nine questions?	Here are our words:
	 "Each argument may be either
	    — empty,
	    — an atom *cons*ed onto a list, or
	    — a list *cons*ed onto a list.
	 For example, at the same time as the first argument may be the empty list, the second argument could be the empty list or have an atom or a list in the *car* position."

Write *eqlist?* using *eqan?*

```
(define eqlist?
  (lambda (l1 l2)
    (cond
      ((and (null? l1) (null? l2)) #t)
      ((and (null? l1) (atom? (car l2)))
       #f)
      ((null? l1) #f)
      ((and (atom? (car l1)) (null? l2))
       #f)
      ((and (atom? (car l1))
            (atom? (car l2)))
       (and (eqan? (car l1) (car l2))
            (eqlist? (cdr l1) (cdr l2))))
      ((atom? (car l1)) #f)
      ((null? l2) #f)
      ((atom? (car l2)) #f)
      (else
        (and (eqlist? (car l1) (car l2))
             (eqlist? (cdr l1) (cdr l2)))))))
```

Is it okay to ask (*atom?* (*car l2*)) in the second question?

Yes, because we know that the second list cannot be empty. Otherwise the first question would have been true.

And why is the third question (*null? l1*)

At that point, we know that when the first argument is empty, the second argument is neither the empty list nor a list with an atom as the first element. If (*null? l1*) is true now, the second argument must be a list whose first element is also a list.

True or false: if the first argument is () *eqlist?* responds with #t in only one case.

True.
For (*eqlist?* (**quote** ()) *l2*) to be true, *l2* must also be the empty list.

Does this mean that the questions
   (**and** (*null? l1*) (*null? l2*))
and
   (**or** (*null? l1*) (*null? l2*))
suffice to determine the answer in the first
three cases?

Yes. If the first question is true, *eqlist?*
responds with #t; otherwise, the answer is
#f.

Rewrite *eqlist?*

```
(define eqlist?
  (lambda (l1 l2)
    (cond
      ((and (null? l1) (null? l2)) #t)
      ((or (null? l1) (null? l2)) #f)
      ((and (atom? (car l1))
            (atom? (car l2)))
       (and (eqan? (car l1) (car l2))
            (eqlist? (cdr l1) (cdr l2))))
      ((or (atom? (car l1))
           (atom? (car l2)))
       #f)
      (else
        (and (eqlist? (car l1) (car l2))
             (eqlist? (cdr l1) (cdr l2)))))))
```

What is an S-expression?

An S-expression is either an atom or a
(possibly empty) list of S-expressions.

How many questions does *equal?* ask to
determine whether two S-expressions are the
same?

Four. The first argument may be an atom or
a list of S-expressions at the same time as
the second argument may be an atom or a
list of S-expresssions.

Write *equal?*

```
(define equal?
  (lambda (s1 s2)
    (cond
      ((and (atom? s1) (atom? s2))
       (eqan? s1 s2))
      ((atom? s1) #f)
      ((atom? s2) #f)
      (else (eqlist? s1 s2)))))
```

Why is the second question (*atom? s1*)	If it is true, we know that the first argument is an atom and the second argument is a list.

And why is the third question (*atom? s2*)	By the time we ask the third question we know that the first argument is not an atom. So all we need to know in order to distinguish between the two remaining cases is whether or not the second argument is an atom. The first argument must be a list.

Can we summarize the second question and the third question as (**or** (*atom? s1*) (*atom? s2*))	Yes, we can!

Simplify *equal?*	```(define equal?` ` (lambda (s1 s2)` ` (cond` ` ((and (atom? s1) (atom? s2))` ` (eqan? s1 s2))` ` ((or (atom? s1) (atom? s2))` ` #f)` ` (else (eqlist? s1 s2))))))```

Does *equal?* ask enough questions?	Yes. The questions cover all four possible cases.

Now, rewrite *eqlist?* using *equal?*	```(define eqlist?` ` (lambda (l1 l2)` ` (cond` ` ((and (null? l1) (null? l2)) #t)` ` ((or (null? l1) (null? l2)) #f)` ` (else` ` (and (equal? (car l1) (car l2))` ` (eqlist? (cdr l1) (cdr l2)))))))```

The Sixth Commandment

Simplify only after the function is correct.

Here is *rember* after we replace *lat* by a list *l* of S-expressions and *a* by any S-expression.

```
(define rember
  (lambda (s l)
    (cond
      ((null? l) (quote ()))
      ((atom? (car l))
       (cond
         ((equal? (car l) s) (cdr l))
         (else (cons (car l)
                 (rember s (cdr l))))))
      (else (cond
              ((equal? (car l) s) (cdr l))
              (else (cons (car l)
                      (rember s
                        (cdr l)))))))))
```

Can we simplify it?

Obviously!

```
(define rember
  (lambda (s l)
    (cond
      ((null? l) (quote ()))
      (else (cond
              ((equal? (car l) s) (cdr l))
              (else (cons (car l)
                      (rember s
                        (cdr l)))))))))
```

And how does that differ?

The function *rember* now removes the first matching S-expression *s* in *l*, instead of the first matching atom *a* in *lat*.

Is *rember* a "star" function now?

No.

Why not?

Because *rember* recurs with the *cdr* of *l* only.

Can *rember* be further simplified?

Yes, the inner (**cond** ...) asks questions that the outer (**cond** ...) could ask!

| Do it! | ```
(define rember
  (lambda (s l)
    (cond
      ((null? l) (quote ()))
      ((equal? (car l) s) (cdr l))
      (else (cons (car l)
              (rember s (cdr l)))))))
``` |

Does this new definition look simpler?

Yes, it does!

And does it work just as well?

Yes, because we knew that all the cases and all the recursions were right before we simplified.

Simplify *insertL* *

We can't. Before we can ask (*eq?* (*car l*) *old*) we need to know that (*car l*) is an atom.

When functions are correct and well-designed, we can think about them easily,

And that saved us this time from getting it wrong.

Can all functions that use *eq?* and = be generalized by replacing *eq?* and = by the function *equal?*

Not quite; this won't work for *eqan?*, but will work for all others. In fact, disregarding the trivial example of *eqan?*, that is exactly what we shall assume.
```

6.
Shadows

Is 1 an arithmetic expression?	Yes.
Is 3 an arithmetic expression?	Yes, of course.
Is 1 + 3 an arithmetic expression?	Yes!
Is 1 + 3 × 4 an arithmetic expression?	Definitely.
Is cookie an arithmetic expression?	Yes. Are you almost ready for one?
And, what about 3 ↑ y + 5	Yes.
What is an arithmetic expression in your words?	In ours: "For the purpose of this chapter, an arithmetic expression is either an atom (including numbers), or two arithmetic expressions combined by +, ×, or ↑."
What is (**quote** a)	a.
What is (**quote** +)	The atom +, not the operation ÷.
What does (**quote** ×) stand for?	The atom ×, not the operation ×.
Is (*eq?* (**quote** a) *y*) true or false where *y* is a	True.
Is (*eq?* *x* *y*) true or false where *x* is a and *y* is a	That's the same question again. And the answer is still true.

Is (n + 3) an arithmetic expression?	Not really, since there are parentheses around n + 3. Our definition of arithmetic expression does not mention parentheses.
Could we think of (n + 3) as an arithmetic expression?	Yes, if we keep in mind that the parentheses are not really there.
What would you call (n + 3)	We call it a representation for n + 3.

Why is (n + 3) a good representation?	Because
	    1. (n + 3) is an S-expression.
	It can therefore serve as an argument for a function.
	    2. It structurally resembles n + 3.

True or false: (*numbered? x*) where *x* is 1	True.
How do you represent $3 + 4 \times 5$	(3 + (4 × 5)).
True or false: (*numbered? y*) where *y* is (3 + (4 ↑ 5))	True.
True or false: (*numbered? z*) where *z* is (2 × **sausage**)	False, because **sausage** is not a number.
What is *numbered?*	It is a function that determines whether a representation of an arithmetic expression contains only numbers besides the +, ×, and ↑.

Now can you write a skeleton for *numbered?*	(**define** *numbered?* 　(**lambda** (*aexp*) 　　(**cond** 　　　(_____ _____) 　　　(_____ _____) 　　　(_____ _____) 　　　(_____ _____))))

is a good guess.

What is the first question?	(*atom? aexp*).

What is (*eq?* (*car* (*cdr aexp*)) (**quote** +))	It is the second question.

Can you guess the third one?	(*eq?* (*car* (*cdr aexp*)) (**quote** ×)) is perfect.

And you must know the fourth one.	(*eq?* (*car* (*cdr aexp*)) (**quote** ↑)), of course.

Should we ask another question about *aexp*	No! So we could replace the previous question by **else**.

Why do we ask four, instead of two, questions about arithmetic expressions? After all, arithmetic expressions like (1 + 3) are lats.	Because we consider (1 + 3) as a representation of an arithmetic expression in list form, not as a list itself. And, an arithmetic expression is either a number, or two arithmetic expressions combined by +, ×, or ↑.

Now you can almost write *numbered?*

Here is our proposal:

```
(define numbered?
  (lambda (aexp)
    (cond
      ((atom? aexp) (number? aexp))
      ((eq? (car (cdr aexp)) (quote +))
       ...)
      ((eq? (car (cdr aexp)) (quote ×))
       ...)
      ((eq? (car (cdr aexp)) (quote ↑))
       ...))))
```

Why do we ask (*number? aexp*) when we know that *aexp* is an atom?

Because we want to know if all arithmetic expressions that are atoms are numbers.

What do we need to know if the *aexp* consists of two arithmetic expressions combined by +

We need to find out whether the two subexpressions are numbered.

In which position is the first subexpression?

It is the *car* of *aexp*.

In which position is the second subexpression?

It is the *car* of the *cdr* of the *cdr* of *aexp*.

So what do we need to ask?

(*numbered?* (*car aexp*)) and
(*numbered?* (*car* (*cdr* (*cdr aexp*)))).
Both must be true.

What is the second answer?

(**and** (*numbered?* (*car aexp*))
  (*numbered?* (*car* (*cdr* (*cdr aexp*)))))

Try *numbered?* again.

```
(define numbered?
  (lambda (aexp)
    (cond
      ((atom? aexp) (number? aexp))
      ((eq? (car (cdr aexp)) (quote +))
       (and (numbered? (car aexp))
         (numbered?
           (car (cdr (cdr aexp))))))
      ((eq? (car (cdr aexp)) (quote ×))
       (and (numbered? (car aexp))
         (numbered?
           (car (cdr (cdr aexp))))))
      ((eq? (car (cdr aexp)) (quote ↑))
       (and (numbered? (car aexp))
         (numbered?
           (car (cdr (cdr aexp)))))))))
```

Since *aexp* was already understood to be an arithmetic expression, could we have written *numbered?* in a simpler way?

Yes:

```
(define numbered?
  (lambda (aexp)
    (cond
      ((atom? aexp) (number? aexp))
      (else
        (and (numbered? (car aexp))
          (numbered?
            (car (cdr (cdr aexp)))))))))
```

Why can we simplify?

Because we know we've got the function right.

What is (*value u*)
where *u* is 13

13.

(*value x*)
where
  x is (1 + 3)

4.

(*value y*) where *y* is (1 + (3 ↑ 4))	82.

(*value z*) where *z* is cookie	No answer.

(*value nexp*) returns what we think is the natural value of a numbered arithmetic expression.	We hope.

How many questions does *value* ask about *nexp*	Four.

Now, let's attempt to write *value*	```
	(define value
	  (lambda (nexp)
	    (cond
	      ((atom? nexp) ...)
	      ((eq? (car (cdr nexp)) (quote +))
	       ...)
	      ((eq? (car (cdr nexp)) (quote ×))
	       ...)
	      (else ...))))
	``

What is the natural value of an arithmetic expression that is a number?	It is just that number.

What is the natural value of an arithmetic expression that consists of two arithmetic expressions combined by +	If we had the natural value of the two subexpressions, we could just add up the two values.

Can you think of a way to get the value of the two subexpressions in (1 + (3 × 4))	Of course, by applying *value* to 1, and applying *value* to (3 × 4).

And in general?	By recurring with *value* on the subexpressions.

Give *value* another try.

```
(define value
  (lambda (nexp)
    (cond
      ((atom? nexp) nexp)
      ((eq? (car (cdr nexp)) (quote +))
       (÷ (value (car nexp))
          (value (car (cdr (cdr nexp))))))
      ((eq? (car (cdr nexp)) (quote ×))
       (× (value (car nexp))
          (value (car (cdr (cdr nexp))))))
      (else
        (↑ (value (car nexp))
           (value
             (car (cdr (cdr nexp)))))))))
```

Can you think of a different representation of arithmetic expressions?	There are several of them.

Could (3 4 +) represent 3 + 4	Yes.

Could (+ 3 4)	Yes.

Or (plus 3 4)	Yes.

Is (+ (× 3 6) (↑ 8 2)) a representation of an arithmetic expression?	Yes.

Try to write the function *value* for a new kind of arithmetic expression that is either:
— a number
— a list of the atom + followed by two arithmetic expressions,
— a list of the atom × followed by two arithmetic expressions, or
— a list of the atom ↑ followed by two arithmetic expressions.
	What about
	
	(**define** *value*
	  (**lambda** (*nexp*)
	    (**cond**
	      ((*atom? nexp*) *nexp*)
	      ((*eq?* (*car nexp*) (**quote** +))
	       (✢ (*value* (*cdr nexp*))
	          (*value* (*cdr* (*cdr nexp*)))))
	      ((*eq?* (*car nexp*) (**quote** ×))
	       (× (*value* (*cdr nexp*))
	          (*value* (*cdr* (*cdr nexp*)))))
	      (**else**
	       (↑ (*value* (*cdr nexp*))
	          (*value* (*cdr* (*cdr nexp*)))))))))

You guessed it.	It's wrong.

Let's try an example.	(+ 1 3).

(*atom? nexp*) where *nexp* is (+ 1 3)	No.

(*eq?* (*car nexp*) (**quote** +)) where *nexp* is (+ 1 3)	Yes.

And now recur.	Yes.

What is (*cdr nexp*) where *nexp* is (+ 1 3)	(1 3).

(1 3) is not our representation of an arithmetic expression.	No, we violated The Seventh Commandment. (1 3) is not a subpart that is a representation of an arithmetic expression! We obviously recurred on a list. But remember, not all lists are representations of arithmetic expressions. We have to recur on subexpressions.
How can we get the first subexpression of a representation of an arithmetic expression?	By taking the *car* of the *cdr*.
Is (*cdr* (*cdr* *nexp*)) an arithmetic expression where *nexp* is (+ 1 3)	No, the *cdr* of the *cdr* is (3), and (3) is not an arithmetic expression.
Again, we were thinking of the list (+ 1 3) instead of the representation of an arithmetic expression.	Taking the *car* of the *cdr* of the *cdr* gets us back on the right track.
What do we mean if we say the *car* of the *cdr* of *nexp*	The first subexpression of the representation of an arithmetic expression.

Let's write a function *1st-sub-exp* for arithmetic expressions.	<pre>(define 1st-sub-exp
	  (lambda (aexp)
	    (cond
	      (else (car (cdr aexp))))))</pre>

Why do we ask **else**	Because the first question is also the last question.

Can we get by without (**cond** ...) if we don't need to ask questions?	Yes, remember one-liners from chapter 4.
	<pre>(define 1st-sub-exp
	  (lambda (aexp)
	    (car (cdr aexp))))</pre>

Write *2nd-sub-exp* for arithmetic expressions.

```
(define 2nd-sub-exp
  (lambda (aexp)
    (car (cdr (cdr aexp)))))
```

Finally, let's replace (*car nexp*) by (*operator nexp*)

```
(define operator
  (lambda (aexp)
    (car aexp)))
```

Now write *value* again.

```
(define value
  (lambda (nexp)
    (cond
      ((atom? nexp) nexp)
      ((eq? (operator nexp) (quote +))
       (⊕ (value (1st-sub-exp nexp))
          (value (2nd-sub-exp nexp))))
      ((eq? (operator nexp) (quote ×))
       (× (value (1st-sub-exp nexp))
          (value (2nd-sub-exp nexp))))
      (else
        (↑ (value (1st-sub-exp nexp))
           (value (2nd-sub-exp nexp)))))))
```

Can we use this *value* function for the first representation of arithmetic expressions in this chapter?

Yes, by changing *1st-sub-exp* and *operator*.

Do it!

```
(define 1st-sub-exp
  (lambda (aexp)
    (car aexp)))
```

```
(define operator
  (lambda (aexp)
    (car (cdr aexp))))
```

Wasn't this easy?	Yes, because we used help functions to hide the representation.

The Eighth Commandment

Use help functions to abstract from representations.

Have we seen representations before?	Yes, we just did not tell you that they were representations.
For what entities have we used representations?	Truth-values! Numbers!
Numbers are representations?	Yes. For example 4 stands for the concept four. We chose that symbol because we are accustomed to arabic representations.
What else could we have used?	(() () () ()) would have served just as well. What about (((((()))))? How about (I V)?
Do you remember how many primitives we need for numbers?	Four: *number?*, *zero?*, *add1*, and *sub1*.
Let's try another representation for numbers. How shall we represent zero now?	() is our choice.
How is one represented?	(()).
How is two represented?	(() ()).

Got it? What's three?	Three is (() () ()).

Write a function to test for zero.	(**define** *sero?*
	  (**lambda** (*n*)
	    (*null? n*)))

Can you write a function that is like *add1*	(**define** *edd1*
	  (**lambda** (*n*)
	    (*cons* (**quote** ()) *n*)))

What about *sub1*	(**define** *zub1*
	  (**lambda** (*n*)
	    (*cdr n*)))

Is this correct?	Let's see.

What is (*zub1 n*) where *n* is ()	No answer, but that's fine. — Recall The Law of Cdr.

Rewrite ✢ using this representation.	(**define** ✢
	  (**lambda** (*n m*)
	    (**cond**
	      ((*sero? m*) *n*)
	      (**else** (*edd1* (✢ *n* (*zub1 m*)))))))

Has the definition of ✢ changed?	Yes and no. It changed, but only slightly.

Recall *lat?*

Easy:

> (**define** *lat?*
>   (**lambda** (*l*)
>   (**cond**
>   ((*null?* *l*) #t)
>   ((*atom?* (*car* *l*)) (*lat?* (*cdr* *l*)))
>   (**else** #f))))

But why did you ask?

Do you remember what the value of (*lat?* *ls*) is where *ls* is (1 2 3)

#t , of course.

What is (1 2 3) with our new numbers?

((()) (()()) (()()())).

What is (*lat?* *ls*) where
   ls is ((()) (()()) (()()()))

It is very false.

Is that bad?

You must beware of shadows.

7.
Friends and Relations

Is this a set? (apple peaches apple plum)	No, since apple appears more than once.

True or false: *(set? lat)* where *lat* is (apples peaches pears plums)	#t , because no atom appears more than once.

How about *(set? lat)* where *lat* is ()	#t , because no atom appears more than once.

Try to write *set?*

```
(define set?
  (lambda (lat)
    (cond
      ((null? lat) #t )
      (else
        (cond
          ((member? (car lat) (cdr lat))
           #f )
          (else (set? (cdr lat)))))))))
```

Simplify *set?*

```
(define set?
  (lambda (lat)
    (cond
      ((null? lat) #t )
      ((member? (car lat) (cdr lat)) #f )
      (else (set? (cdr lat))))))
```

Does this work for the example (apple 3 pear 4 9 apple 3 4)	Yes, since *member?* is now written using *equal?* instead of *eq?*.

Were you surprised to see the function *member?* appear in the definition of *set?*	You should not be, because we have written *member?* already, and now we can use it whenever we want.

What is (*makeset lat*)
where
   lat is (apple peach pear peach
        plum apple lemon peach)

(apple peach pear plum lemon).

Try to write *makeset* using *member?*

```
(define makeset
  (lambda (lat)
    (cond
      ((null? lat) (quote ()))
      ((member? (car lat) (cdr lat))
       (makeset (cdr lat)))
      (else (cons (car lat)
              (makeset (cdr lat)))))))
```

Are you surprised to see how short this is?

We hope so. But don't be afraid: it's right.

Using the previous definition, what is the result of (*makeset lat*)
where
   lat is (apple peach pear peach
        plum apple lemon peach)

(pear plum apple lemon peach).

Try to write *makeset* using *multirember*

```
(define makeset
  (lambda (lat)
    (cond
      ((null? lat) (quote ()))
      (else (cons (car lat)
              (makeset
                (multirember (car lat)
                  (cdr lat))))))))
```

What is the result of (*makeset lat*) using this second definition
where
   lat is (apple peach pear peach
        plum apple lemon peach)

(apple peach pear plum lemon).

Describe in your own words how the second definition of *makeset* works.

Here are our words:
"The function *makeset* remembers to *cons* the first atom in the lat onto the result of the natural recursion, after removing all occurrences of the first atom from the rest of the lat."

Does the second *makeset* work for the example

(apple 3 pear 4 9 apple 3 4)

Yes, since *multirember* is now written using *equal?* instead of *eq?*.

What is (*subset? set1 set2*)
where
   set1 is (5 chicken wings)
and
   set2 is (5 hamburgers
         2 pieces fried chicken and
         light duckling wings)

#t , because each atom in *set1* is also in *set2*.

What is (*subset? set1 set2*)
where
   set1 is (4 pounds of horseradish)
and
   set2 is (four pounds chicken and
         5 ounces horseradish)

#f.

Write *subset?*

```
(define subset?
  (lambda (set1 set2)
    (cond
      ((null? set1) #t)
      (else (cond
              ((member? (car set1) set2)
               (subset? (cdr set1) set2))
              (else #f))))))
```

Can you write a shorter version of *subset?*

```
(define subset?
  (lambda (set1 set2)
    (cond
      ((null? set1) #t)
      ((member? (car set1) set2)
       (subset? (cdr set1) set2))
      (else #f))))
```

Try to write *subset?* with (**and** ...)

```
(define subset?
  (lambda (set1 set2)
    (cond
      ((null? set1) #t)
      (else
        (and (member? (car set1) set2)
             (subset? (cdr set1) set2))))))
```

What is (*eqset? set1 set2*)
where
    set1 is (6 large chickens with wings)
and
    set2 is (6 chickens with large wings)

#t.

Write *eqset?*

```
(define eqset?
  (lambda (set1 set2)
    (cond
      ((subset? set1 set2)
       (subset? set2 set1))
      (else #f))))
```

Can you write *eqset?* with only one
cond-line?

```
(define eqset?
  (lambda (set1 set2)
    (cond
      (else (and (subset? set1 set2)
                 (subset? set2 set1))))))
```

Write the one-liner.

```
(define eqset?
  (lambda (set1 set2)
    (and (subset? set1 set2)
         (subset? set2 set1))))
```

What is (intersect? set1 set2)
where
   set1 is (stewed tomatoes and macaroni)
and
   set2 is (macaroni and cheese)

#t,
because at least one atom in set1 is in set2.

Define the function intersect?

```
(define intersect?
  (lambda (set1 set2)
    (cond
      ((null? set1) #f)
      (else
        (cond
          ((member? (car set1) set2) #t)
          (else (intersect?
                  (cdr set1) set2)))))))
```

Write the shorter version.

```
(define intersect?
  (lambda (set1 set2)
    (cond
      ((null? set1) #f)
      ((member? (car set1) set2) #t)
      (else (intersect? (cdr set1) set2)))))
```

Try writing intersect? with (or ...)

```
(define intersect?
  (lambda (set1 set2)
    (cond
      ((null? set1) #f)
      (else (or (member? (car set1) set2)
                (intersect?
                  (cdr set1) set2))))))
```

Compare subset? and intersect?.

What is (*intersect set1 set2*)
where
   set1 is (stewed tomatoes and macaroni)
and
   set2 is (macaroni and cheese)

(and macaroni).

Now you can write the short version of
intersect

```
(define intersect
  (lambda (set1 set2)
    (cond
      ((null? set1) (quote ()))
      ((member? (car set1) set2)
       (cons (car set1)
         (intersect (cdr set1) set2)))
      (else (intersect (cdr set1) set2)))))
```

What is (*union set1 set2*)
where
   set1 is (stewed tomatoes and
         macaroni casserole)
and
   set2 is (macaroni and cheese)

(stewed tomatoes casserole macaroni
 and cheese)

Write *union*

```
(define union
  (lambda (set1 set2)
    (cond
      ((null? set1) set2)
      ((member? (car set1) set2)
       (union (cdr set1) set2))
      (else (cons (car set1)
              (union (cdr set1) set2))))))
```

What is this function?

```
(define xxx
  (lambda (set1 set2)
    (cond
      ((null? set1) (quote ()))
      ((member? (car set1) set2)
       (xxx (cdr set1) set2))
      (else (cons (car set1)
                  (xxx (cdr set1) set2))))))
```

In our words:
  "It is a function that returns all the atoms
   in *set1* that are not in *set2*."
That is, *xxx* is the (set) difference function.

What is (*intersectall l-set*)
where
  l-set is ((a b c) (c a d e) (e f g h a b))

(a).

What is (*intersectall l-set*)
where
  l-set is ((6 pears and)
             (3 peaches and 6 peppers)
             (8 pears and 6 plums)
             (and 6 prunes with some apples))

(6 and).

Now, using whatever help functions you
need, write *intersectall* assuming that the list
of sets is non-empty.

```
(define intersectall
  (lambda (l-set)
    (cond
      ((null? (cdr l-set)) (car l-set))
      (else (intersect (car l-set)
                       (intersectall (cdr l-set)))))))
```

Is this a pair?[1]
  (pear pear)

Yes, because it is a list with only two atoms.

---

[1] A pair in Scheme (or Lisp) is a different but related object.

Is this a pair? (3 7)	Yes.

Is this a pair? ((2) (pair))	Yes, because it is a list with only two S-expressions.

(*a-pair? l*)
where
  l is (full (house))
	#t ,
	  because it is a list with only two
	  S-expressions.

Define *a-pair?*	```
	(define a-pair?
	  (lambda (x)
	    (cond
	      ((atom? x) #f)
	      ((null? x) #f)
	      ((null? (cdr x)) #f)
	      ((null? (cdr (cdr x))) #t)
	      (else #f))))
	``

How can you refer to the first S-expression of a pair?	By taking the *car* of the pair.

How can you refer to the second S-expression of a pair?	By taking the *car* of the *cdr* of the pair.

How can you build a pair with two atoms?	You *cons* the first one onto the *cons* of the second one onto (). That is, (*cons x1* (*cons x2* (**quote** ())))).

How can you build a pair with two S-expressions?	You *cons* the first one onto the *cons* of the second one onto (). That is, (*cons x1* (*cons x2* (**quote** ())))).

Did you notice the differences between the last two answers?	No, there aren't any.

```
(define first
  (lambda (p)
    (cond
      (else (car p)))))
```

```
(define second
  (lambda (p)
    (cond
      (else (car (cdr p))))))
```

```
(define build
  (lambda (s1 s2)
    (cond
      (else (cons s1
                (cons s2 (quote ())))))))
```

What possible uses do these three functions have?

They are used to make representations of pairs and to get parts of representations of pairs. See chapter 6.

They will be used to improve readability, as you will soon see.

Redefine *first*, *second*, and *build* as one-liners.

Can you write *third* as a one-liner?

```
(define third
  (lambda (l)
    (car (cdr (cdr l)))))
```

Is *l* a rel where
   l is (apples peaches pumpkin pie)

No, since *l* is not a list of pairs. We use rel to stand for relation.

Is *l* a rel where
   l is ((apples peaches)
     (pumpkin pie)
     (apples peaches))

No, since *l* is not a set of pairs.

Is *l* a rel where
   l is ((apples peaches) (pumpkin pie))

Yes.

Is *l* a rel where
   l is ((4 3) (4 2) (7 6) (6 2) (3 4))

Yes.

Is *rel* a fun where *rel* is ((4 3) (4 2) (7 6) (6 2) (3 4))	No. We use fun to stand for function.

What is (*fun? rel*)
where
  rel is ((8 3) (4 2) (7 6) (6 2) (3 4))
	#t , because (*firsts rel*) is a set
	  —See chapter 3.

What is (*fun? rel*) where *rel* is ((d 4) (b 0) (b 9) (e 5) (g 4))	#f, because b is repeated.

Write *fun?* with *set?* and *firsts*

```
(define fun?
  (lambda (rel)
    (set? (firsts rel))))
```

Is *fun?* a simple one-liner?	It sure is.

How do we represent a finite function?	For us, a finite function is a list of pairs in which no first element of any pair is the same as any other first element.

What is (*revrel rel*) where *rel* is ((8 a) (pumpkin pie) (got sick))	((a 8) (pie pumpkin) (sick got)).

You can now write *revrel*

```
(define revrel
  (lambda (rel)
    (cond
      ((null? rel) (quote ()))
      (else (cons (build
                    (second (car rel))
                    (first (car rel)))
              (revrel (cdr rel)))))))
```

Would the following also be correct:

```
(define revrel
  (lambda (rel)
    (cond
      ((null? rel) (quote ()))
      (else (cons (cons
                    (car (cdr (car rel)))
                    (cons (car (car rel))
                      (quote ())))
              (revrel (cdr rel)))))))
```

Yes, but now do you see how representation aids readability?

Suppose we had the function *revpair* that reversed the two components of a pair like this:

```
(define revpair
  (lambda (pair)
    (build (second pair) (first pair))))
```

How would you rewrite *revrel* to use this help function?

No problem, and it is even easier to read:

```
(define revrel
  (lambda (rel)
    (cond
      ((null? rel) (quote ()))
      (else (cons (revpair (car rel))
              (revrel (cdr rel)))))))
```

Can you guess why *fun* is not a fullfun where

   fun is ((8 3) (4 2) (7 6) (6 2) (3 4))

fun is not a fullfun, since the 2 appears more than once as a second item of a pair.

Why is #t the value of (*fullfun? fun*) where

   fun is ((8 3) (4 8) (7 6) (6 2) (3 4))

Because (3 8 6 2 4) is a set.

What is (*fullfun? fun*) where
   fun is ((grape raisin)
          (plum prune)
          (stewed prune))

#f.

What is (*fullfun? fun*)
where
   fun is ((grape raisin)
         (plum prune)
         (stewed grape))
	#t , because (raisin prune grape) is a set.

Define *fullfun?*

```
(define fullfun?
  (lambda (fun)
    (set? (seconds fun))))
```

Can you define *seconds*	It is just like *firsts*.

What is another name for *fullfun?*	*one-to-one?*.

Can you think of a second way to write
one-to-one?

```
(define one-to-one?
  (lambda (fun)
    (fun? (revrel fun))))
```

Is ((chocolate chip) (doughy cookie)) a one-to-one function?	Yes, and you deserve one now!

Go and get one!

Or better yet, make your own.

```
(define cookies
  (lambda ()
    (bake
       (quote (350 degrees))
       (quote (12 minutes))
       (mix
          (quote (walnuts 1 cup))
          (quote (chocolate-chips 16 ounces))
          (mix
             (mix
                (quote (flour 2 cups))
                (quote (oatmeal 2 cups))
                (quote (salt .5 teaspoon))
                (quote (baking-powder 1 teaspoon))
                (quote (baking-soda 1 teaspoon)))
          (mix
             (quote (eggs 2 large))
             (quote (vanilla 1 teaspoon))
             (cream
                (quote (butter 1 cup))
                (quote (sugar 2 cups)))))))))
```

8.
Lambda the Ultimate

Remember what we did in *rember* and *insertL* at the end of chapter 5?	We replaced *eq?* with *equal?*
Can you write a function *rember-f* that would use either *eq?* or *equal?*	No, because we have not yet told you how.
How can you make *rember* remove the first a from (b c a)	By passing a and (b c a) as arguments to *rember*.
How can you make *rember* remove the first c from (b c a)	By passing c and (b c a) as arguments to *rember*.
How can you make *rember-f* use *equal?* instead of *eq?*	By passing *equal?* as an argument to *rember-f*.

What is (*rember-f test? a l*)
where
    test? is $=$[1]
    a is 5
and
    l is (6 2 5 3)
	(6 2 3).

[1] L: `(rember-f (function =) 5 '(6 2 5 3))`, but there is more.

What is (*rember-f test? a l*)
where
    test? is *eq?*
    a is jelly
and
    l is (jelly beans are good)
	(beans are good).

And what is (*rember-f test? a l*)
where
    test? is *equal?*
    a is (pop corn)
and
    l is (lemonade (pop corn) and (cake))
	(lemonade and (cake)).

Try to write *rember-f*

```
(define rember-f
  (lambda (test? a l)
    (cond
      ((null? l) (quote ()))
      (else (cond
              ((test? (car l) a)¹ (cdr l))
              (else (cons (car l)
                      (rember-f test? a
                        (cdr l)))))))))
```

This is good!

---

¹ L: (funcall test? (car l) a). Use funcall when
invoking a function argument or a function that has not
been **defun**ed.

What about the short version?

```
(define rember-f
  (lambda (test? a l)
    (cond
      ((null? l) (quote ()))
      ((test? (car l) a) (cdr l))
      (else (cons (car l)
              (rember-f test? a
                (cdr l)))))))
```

How does (*rember-f test? a l*) act
where *test?* is *eq?*

(*rember-f test? a l*)
where *test?* is *eq?*, acts like *rember*.

And what about (*rember-f test? a l*)
where *test?* is *equal?*

This is just *rember* with *eq?* replaced by
equal?.

Now we have four functions that do almost
the same thing.

Yes:
  rember with =
  rember with *equal?*
  rember with *eq?*
and
  rember-f.

And *rember-f* can behave like all the others.	Let's generate all versions with *rember-f*.
What kind of values can functions return?	Lists and atoms.
What about functions themselves?	Yes, but you probably did not know that yet.
Can you say what (**lambda** $(a\ l)$ ...) is?	(**lambda** $(a\ l)$ ...) is a function of two arguments, a and l.

Now what is
    (**lambda** (a)
        (**lambda** (x)
            $(eq?\ x\ a)))$
	It is a function that, when passed an argument a, returns the function
	
	    (**lambda** (x)
	        $(eq?\ x\ a))$
	
	where a is just that argument.

Is this called "Curry-ing?"	Thank you, Moses Schönfinkel (1889–1942).
It is not called "Schönfinkel-ing."	Thank you, Haskell B. Curry (1900–1982).

Using (**define** ...) give the preceding function a name.	(**define** *eq?-c*[1]
	    (**lambda** (a)
	        (**lambda** (x)
	            $(eq?\ x\ a))))$
	
	This is our choice.

[1] L: (defun eq?-c (a)
        (function
            (lambda (x)
                (eq x a))))

What is $(eq?\text{-}c\ k)$ where k is salad	Its value is a function that takes x as an argument and tests whether it is *eq?* to salad.

So let's give it a name using (**define** ...)   Okay.

> (**define**[1] *eq?-salad* (*eq?-c k*))

where *k* is salad

---

[1] L: `(setq eq?-salad (eq?-c 'salad))`.
Use `setq` to define a function that can be `funcalled`.

What is (*eq?-salad y*)[1]   #t.
where *y* is salad

---

[1] L: `(funcall eq?-salad y)`, since `eq?-salad` has not been
`defuned`.

And what is (*eq?-salad y*)   #f.
where *y* is tuna

Do we need to give a name to *eq?-salad*   No, we may just as well ask
                                                  ((*eq?-c x*) *y*)[1]
                                                where
                                                  x is salad
                                                and
                                                  y is tuna.

---

[1] L: `(funcall (eq?-c x) y)`, since `(eq?-c x)` is a function
that has not been `defuned`.

Now rewrite *rember-f* as a function of one
argument *test?* that returns an argument like
rember with *eq?* replaced by *test?*

> (**define** *rember-f*
>   (**lambda** (*test?*)
>   (**lambda** (*a l*)
>   (**cond**
>   ((*null? l*) (**quote** ()))
>   ((*test?* (*car l*) *a*) (*cdr l*))
>   (**else** (*cons* (*car l*) ...))))))

is a good start.

Describe in your own words the result of
   (*rember-f test?*)
where
   test? is *eq?*

It is a function that takes two arguments, *a* and *l*. It compares the elements of the list with *a*, and the first one that is *eq?* to *a* is removed.

Give a name to the function returned by
   (*rember-f test?*)
where
   test? is *eq?*

> (**define** *rember-eq?* (*rember-f test?*))

where
   test? is *eq?*.

What is (*rember-eq? a l*)
where *a* is tuna
and
   l is (tuna salad is good)

(salad is good).

Did we need to give the name *rember-eq?* to the function (*rember-f test?*)
where
   test? is *eq?*

No, we could have written
   ((*rember-f test?*) *a l*)
where
   test? is *eq?*
   a is tuna
and
   l is (tuna salad is good).

Now, complete the line
   (*cons* (*car l*) ...)
in *rember-f* so that *rember-f* works.

```
(define rember-f
  (lambda (test?)
    (lambda (a l)
      (cond
        ((null? l) (quote ()))
        ((test? (car l) a) (cdr l))
        (else (cons (car l)
                ((rember-f test?) a
                  (cdr l)))))))))
```

What is ((*rember-f eq?*) *a l*)
where *a* is tuna
and
   l is (shrimp salad and tuna salad)

(shrimp salad and salad).

What is ((*rember-f eq?*) *a l*)
where *a* is eq?
and
   l is (equal? eq? eqan? eqlist? eqpair?)[1]

(equal? eqan? eqlist? eqpair?).

---

[1] Did you notice the difference between eq? and *eq*? Remember that the former is the atom and the latter is the function.

And now transform *insertL* to *insertL-f* the same way we have transformed *rember* into *rember-f*

```
(define insertL-f
  (lambda (test?)
    (lambda (new old l)
      (cond
        ((null? l) (quote ()))
        ((test? (car l) old)
         (cons new (cons old (cdr l))))
        (else (cons (car l)
                    ((insertL-f test?) new old
                     (cdr l))))))))
```

And, just for the exercise, do it to *insertR*

```
(define insertR-f
  (lambda (test?)
    (lambda (new old l)
      (cond
        ((null? l) (quote ()))
        ((test? (car l) old)
         (cons old (cons new (cdr l))))
        (else (cons (car l)
                    ((insertR-f test?) new old
                     (cdr l))))))))
```

Are *insertR* and *insertL* similar?

Only the middle piece is a bit different.

Can you write a function *insert-g* that would insert either at the left or at the right?

If you can, get yourself some coffee cake and relax! Otherwise, don't give up. You'll see it in a minute.

Chapter 8

Which pieces differ?	The second lines differ from each other. In *insertL* it is: $\quad((eq?\ (car\ l)\ old)$ $\quad\ (cons\ new\ (cons\ old\ (cdr\ l)))),$ but in *insertR* it is: $\quad((eq?\ (car\ l)\ old)$ $\quad\ (cons\ old\ (cons\ new\ (cdr\ l)))).$

Put the difference in words!	We say: "The two functions *cons old* and *new* in a different order onto the *cdr* of the list *l*."

So how can we get rid of the difference?	You probably guessed it: by passing in a function that expresses the appropriate *cons*ing.

| Define a function *seqL* that<br>  1. takes three arguments, and<br>  2. *cons*es the first argument<br>     onto the result of *cons*ing<br>     the second argument onto<br>     the third argument. | ```
(define seqL
  (lambda (new old l)
    (cons new (cons old l))))
``` |

| What is:<br><br>```
(define seqR
  (lambda (new old l)
    (cons old (cons new l))))
``` | A function that<br>  1. takes three arguments, and<br>  2. *cons*es the second argument<br>     onto the result of *cons*ing<br>     the first argument onto<br>     the third argument. |

Do you know why we wrote these functions?	Because they express what the two differing lines in *insertL* and *insertR* express.

Try to write the function *insert-g* of one
argument *seq*
   which returns *insertL*
      where *seq* is *seqL*
and
   which returns *insertR*
      where *seq* is *seqR*

```
(define insert-g
  (lambda (seq)
    (lambda (new old l)
      (cond
        ((null? l) (quote ()))
        ((eq? (car l) old)
         (seq new old (cdr l)))
        (else (cons (car l)
                    ((insert-g seq) new old
                     (cdr l))))))))
```

Now define *insertL* with *insert-g*

```
(define insertL (insert-g seqL))
```

And *insertR*.

```
(define insertR (insert-g seqR))
```

Is there something unusual about these two
definitions?

Yes. Earlier we would probably have written
    (**define** *insertL* (*insert-g seq*))
where
  seq is *seqL*
and
    (**define** *insertR* (*insert-g seq*))
where
  seq is *seqR*.
But, using "where" is unnecessary when you
pass functions as arguments.

Is it necessary to give names to *seqL* and
seqR

Not really. We could have passed their
definitions instead.

Define *insertL* again with *insert-g*
Do not pass in *seqL* this time.

```
(define insertL
  (insert-g
    (lambda (new old l)
      (cons new (cons old l)))))
```

Is this better?

Yes, because you do not need to remember as many names. You can

(*rember func-name* "your-mind")

where *func-name* is *seqL*.

Do you remember the definition of *subst*

Here is one.

```
(define subst
  (lambda (new old l)
    (cond
      ((null? l) (quote ()))
      ((eq? (car l) old)
       (cons new (cdr l)))
      (else (cons (car l)
                  (subst new old (cdr l)))))))
```

Does this look familiar?

Yes, it looks like *insertL* or *insertR*. Just the answer of the second **cond**-line is different.

Define a function like *seqL* or *seqR* for *subst*

What do you think about this?

```
(define seqS
  (lambda (new old l)
    (cons new l)))
```

And now define *subst* using *insert-g*

```
(define subst (insert-g seqS))
```

And what do you think *yyy* is

```
(define yyy
  (lambda (a l)
    ((insert-g seqrem) #f a l)))
```

where

```
(define seqrem
  (lambda (new old l)
    l))
```

Surprise! It is our old friend *rember*

Hint: Step through the evaluation of
  (*yyy a l*)
where
  a is sausage
and
  l is (pizza with sausage and bacon).
What role does #f play?

What you have just seen is the power of abstraction.

The Ninth Commandment

Abstract common patterns with a new function.

Have we seen similar functions before?	Yes, we have even seen functions with similar lines.

Do you remember *value* from chapter 6?

```
(define value
  (lambda (nexp)
    (cond
      ((atom? nexp) nexp)
      ((eq? (operator nexp)
            (quote +))
       (✢ (value (1st-sub-exp nexp))
          (value (2nd-sub-exp nexp))))
      ((eq? (operator nexp)
            (quote ×))
       (× (value (1st-sub-exp nexp))
          (value (2nd-sub-exp nexp))))
      (else
        (↑ (value (1st-sub-exp nexp))
           (value (2nd-sub-exp nexp)))))))
```

Do you see the similarities?	The last three answers are the same except for the ✢, ×, and ↑.

Can you write the function *atom-to-function* which:
1. Takes one argument x and
2. returns the function ✢
   if (*eq?* x (**quote** +))
   returns the function ×
   if (*eq?* x (**quote** ×)) and
   returns the function ↑
   otherwise?

```
(define atom-to-function
  (lambda (x)
    (cond
      ((eq? x (quote +)) ✢ )
      ((eq? x (quote ×)) ×)
      (else ↑))))
```

What is (*atom-to-function* (*operator nexp*)) where *nexp* is (+ 5 3)	The function ⊹, not the atom +.

Can you use *atom-to-function* to rewrite *value* with only two **cond**-lines?	Of course.

```
(define value
  (lambda (nexp)
    (cond
      ((atom? nexp) nexp)
      (else
        ((atom-to-function
          (operator nexp))
         (value (1st-sub-exp nexp))
         (value (2nd-sub-exp nexp)))))))
```

Is this quite a bit shorter than the first version?	Yes, but that's okay. We haven't changed its meaning.

Time for an apple?	One a day keeps the doctor away.

Here is *multirember* again.	No problem.

```
(define multirember
  (lambda (a lat)
    (cond
      ((null? lat) (quote ()))
      ((eq? (car lat) a)
       (multirember a (cdr lat)))
      (else (cons (car lat)
              (multirember a
                (cdr lat)))))))
```

```
(define multirember-f
  (lambda (test?)
    (lambda (a lat)
      (cond
        ((null? lat) (quote ()))
        ((test? a (car lat))
         ((multirember-f test?) a
          (cdr lat)))
        (else (cons (car lat)
                ((multirember-f test?) a
                 (cdr lat))))))))
```

Write *multirember-f*

What is ((*multirember-f test?*) *a lat*) where
   test? is *eq?*
   a is tuna
and
   lat is (shrimp salad tuna salad and tuna)
	(shrimp salad salad and).

Wasn't that easy?	Yes.

Define *multirember-eq?* using *multirember-f*

> (**define** *multirember-eq?*
>   (*multirember-f test?*))

where *test?* is *eq?*.

Do we really need to tell *multirember-f* about tuna

As *multirember-f* visits all the elements in *lat*, it always looks for tuna.

Does *test?* change as *multirember-f* goes through *lat*

No, *test?* always stands for *eq?*, just as *a* always stands for tuna.

Can we combine *a* and *test?*

Well, *test?* could be a function of just one argument and could compare that argument to tuna.

How would it do that?

The new *test?* takes one argument and compares it to tuna.

Here is one way to write this function.

> (**define** *eq?-tuna*
>   (*eq?-c k*))

where *k* is tuna
Can you think of a different way of writing this function?

Yes, and here is a different way:

> (**define** *eq?-tuna*
>   (*eq?-c* (**quote** tuna)))

Have you ever seen definitions that contain atoms?

Yes, 0, (**quote** ×), (**quote** +), and many more.

Perhaps we should now write *multirememberT* which is similar to *multirember-f* Instead of taking *test?* and returning a function, *multirememberT* takes a function like *eq?-tuna* and a lat and then does its work.

This is not really difficult.

```
(define multirememberT
  (lambda (test? lat)
    (cond
      ((null? lat) (quote ()))
      ((test? (car lat))
       (multirememberT test? (cdr lat)))
      (else (cons (car lat)
              (multirememberT test?
                (cdr lat)))))))
```

What is (*multirememberT test? lat*)
where
  test? is *eq?-tuna*
and
  lat is (shrimp salad tuna salad and tuna)

(shrimp salad salad and).

Is this easy?

It's not bad.

How about this?

Now that looks really complicated!

```
(define multirember&co
  (lambda (a lat col)
    (cond
      ((null? lat)
       (col (quote ()) (quote ())))
      ((eq? (car lat) a)
       (multirember&co a
         (cdr lat)
         (lambda (newlat seen)
           (col newlat
             (cons (car lat) seen)))))
      (else
        (multirember&co a
          (cdr lat)
          (lambda (newlat seen)
            (col (cons (car lat) newlat)
              seen)))))))
```

Here is something simpler:

> (**define** *a-friend*
>   (**lambda** (*x y*)
>   (*null? y*)))

Yes, it is simpler. It is a function that takes two arguments and asks whether the second one is the empty list. It ignores its first argument.

What is the value of
    (*multirember&co a lat col*)
where
    a is tuna
    lat is (strawberries tuna and swordfish)
and
    col is *a-friend*

This is not simple.

So let's try a friendlier example. What is the value of (*multirember&co a lat col*)
where
    a is tuna
    lat is ()
and
    col is *a-friend*

#t , because *a-friend* is immediately used in the first answer on two empty lists, and *a-friend* makes sure that its second argument is empty.

And what is (*multirember&co a lat col*)
where
    a is tuna
    lat is (tuna)
and
    col is *a-friend*

multirember&co asks
    (*eq?* (*car lat*) (**quote** tuna))
where
    lat is (tuna).
Then it recurs on ().

What are the other arguments that *multirember&co* uses for the natural recursion?

The first one is clearly tuna. The third argument is a new function.

What is the name of the third argument?

col.

Do you know what *col* stands for?

The name *col* is short for "collector." A collector is sometimes called a "continuation."

Here is the new collector:

```
(define new-friend
  (lambda (newlat seen)
    (col newlat
      (cons (car lat) seen))))
```

where
  (car lat) is tuna
and
  col is a-friend

Can you write this definition differently?

Do you mean the new way where we put tuna into the definition?

```
(define new-friend
  (lambda (newlat seen)
    (col newlat
      (cons (quote tuna) seen))))
```

where
  col is a-friend.

Can we also replace col with a-friend in such definitions because col is to a-friend what (car lat) is to tuna

Yes, we can:

```
(define new-friend
  (lambda (newlat seen)
    (a-friend newlat
      (cons (quote tuna) seen))))
```

And now?

multirember&co finds out that (null? lat) is true, which means that it uses the collector on two empty lists.

Which collector is this?

It is new-friend.

How does a-friend differ from new-friend

new-friend uses a-friend on the empty list and the value of
  (cons (quote tuna) (quote ())).

And what does the old collector do with such arguments?

It answers #f, because its second argument is (tuna), which is not the empty list.

What is the value of
  (multirember&co a lat a-friend)
where a is tuna
and
  lat is (and tuna)

This time around multirember&co recurs with yet another friend.

```
(define latest-friend
  (lambda (newlat seen)
    (a-friend (cons (quote and) newlat)
      seen)))
```

And what is the value of this recursive use of *multirember&co*

#f, since (*a-friend ls1 ls2*)
where
   ls1 is (and)
and
   ls2 is (tuna)
is #f.

What does (*multirember&co a lat f*) do?

It looks at every atom of the *lat* to see whether it is *eq?* to a. Those atoms that are not are collected in one list *ls1*; the others for which the answer is true are collected in a second list *ls2*. Finally, it determines the value of (*f ls1 ls2*).

Final question: What is the value of (*multirember&co* (**quote** tuna) *ls col*)
where
   ls is (strawberries tuna and swordfish)
and
   col is

> (**define** *last-friend*
>   (**lambda** (*x y*)
>   (*length x*)))

3, because *ls* contains three things that are not tuna, and therefore *last-friend* is used on (strawberries and swordfish) and (tuna).

Yes!

It's a strange meal, but we have seen foreign foods before.

The Tenth Commandment

Build functions to collect more than one value at a time.

Here is an old friend.

```
(define multiinsertL
  (lambda (new old lat)
    (cond
      ((null? lat) (quote ()))
      ((eq? (car lat) old)
       (cons new
         (cons old
           (multiinsertL new old
             (cdr lat)))))
      (else (cons (car lat)
             (multiinsertL new old
               (cdr lat)))))))
```

Do you also remember *multiinsertR*

No problem.

```
(define multiinsertR
  (lambda (new old lat)
    (cond
      ((null? lat) (quote ()))
      ((eq? (car lat) old)
       (cons old
         (cons new
           (multiinsertR new old
             (cdr lat)))))
      (else (cons (car lat)
             (multiinsertR new old
               (cdr lat)))))))
```

Now try *multiinsertLR*

Hint: *multiinsertLR* inserts *new* to the left of *oldL* and to the right of *oldR* in *lat* if *oldL* are *oldR* are different.

This is a way of combining the two functions.

```
(define multiinsertLR
  (lambda (new oldL oldR lat)
    (cond
      ((null? lat) (quote ()))
      ((eq? (car lat) oldL)
       (cons new
         (cons oldL
           (multiinsertLR new oldL oldR
             (cdr lat)))))
      ((eq? (car lat) oldR)
       (cons oldR
         (cons new
           (multiinsertLR new oldL oldR
             (cdr lat)))))
      (else
        (cons (car lat)
          (multiinsertLR new oldL oldR
            (cdr lat)))))))
```

The function *multiinsertLR&co* is to *multiinsertLR* what *multirember&co* is to *multirember*

Does this mean that *multiinsertLR&co* takes one more argument than *multiinsertLR*?

Yes, and what kind of argument is it?

It is a collector function.

When *multiinsertLR&co* is done, it will use *col* on the new lat, on the number of *left* insertions, and the number of *right* insertions. Can you write an outline of *multiinsertLR&co*

Sure, it is just like *multiinsertLR*.

```
(define multiinsertLR&co
  (lambda (new oldL oldR lat col)
    (cond
      ((null? lat)
       (col (quote ()) 0 0))
      ((eq? (car lat) oldL)
       (multiinsertLR&co new oldL oldR
         (cdr lat)
         (lambda (newlat L R)
           ...)))
      ((eq? (car lat) oldR)
       (multiinsertLR&co new oldL oldR
         (cdr lat)
         (lambda (newlat L R)
           ...)))
      (else
       (multiinsertLR&co new oldL oldR
         (cdr lat)
         (lambda (newlat L R)
           ...))))))) 
```

Why is *col* used on (**quote** ()) 0 and 0 when (*null? lat*) is true?

The empty *lat* contains neither *oldL* nor *oldR*. And this means that 0 occurrences of *oldL* and 0 occurrences of *oldR* are found and that *multiinsertLR* will return () when *lat* is empty.

So what is the value of
(*multiinsertLR&co*
  (**quote** cranberries)
  (**quote** fish)
  (**quote** chips)
  (**quote** ())
  col)

It is the value of (*col* (**quote** ()) 0 0), which we cannot determine because we don't know what *col* is.

Is it true that *multiinsertLR&co* will use the new collector on three arguments when (*car lat*) is equal to neither *oldL* nor *oldR*

Yes, the first is the lat that *multiinsertLR* would have produced for (*cdr lat*), *oldL*, and *oldR*. The second and third are the number of insertions that occurred to the left and right of *oldL* and *oldR*, respectively.

Is it true that *multiinsertLR&co* then uses the function *col* on (*cons* (*car lat*) *newlat*) because it copies the list unless an *oldL* or an *oldR* appears?

Yes, it is true, so we know what the new collector for the last case is:

> (**lambda** (*newlat L R*)
>   (*col* (*cons* (*car lat*) *newlat*) *L R*)).

Why are *col*'s second and third arguments just *L* and *R*

If (*car lat*) is neither *oldL* nor *oldR*, we do not need to insert any new elements. So, *L* and *R* are the correct results for both (*cdr lat*) and all of *lat*.

Here is what we have so far. And we have even thrown in an extra collector:

```
(define multiinsertLR&co
  (lambda (new oldL oldR lat col)
    (cond
      ((null? lat)
       (col (quote ()) 0 0))
      ((eq? (car lat) oldL)
       (multiinsertLR&co new oldL oldR
         (cdr lat)
         (lambda (newlat L R)
           (col (cons new
                   (cons oldL newlat))
             (add1 L) R))))
      ((eq? (car lat) oldR)
       (multiinsertLR&co new oldL oldR
         (cdr lat)
         (lambda (newlat L R)
           ...)))
      (else
        (multiinsertLR&co new oldL oldR
          (cdr lat)
          (lambda (newlat L R)
            (col (cons (car lat) newlat)
              L R)))))))
```

Can you fill in the dots?

The incomplete collector is similar to the extra collector. Instead of adding one to *L*, it adds one to *R*, and instead of *consing new* onto *consing oldL* onto *newlat*, it *conses oldR* onto the result of *consing new* onto *newlat*.

So can you fill in the dots?

Yes, the final collector is

> (**lambda** (*newlat L R*)
>   (*col* (*cons oldR* (*cons new newlat*))
>   *L* (*add1 R*))).

What is the value of
(*multiinsertLR&co new oldL oldR lat col*)
where
   new is salty
   oldL is fish
   oldR is chips
and
   lat is (chips and fish or fish and chips)

It is the value of (*col newlat* 2 2)
where
   newlat is (chips salty and salty fish
              or salty fish and chips salty).

Is this healthy?

Looks like lots of salt. Perhaps dessert is sweeter.

Do you remember what *-functions are?

Yes, all *-functions work on lists that are either
   — empty,
   — an atom *cons*ed onto a list, or
   — a list *cons*ed onto a list.

Now write the function *evens-only** which removes all odd numbers from a list of nested lists. Here is *even?*

```
(define even?
  (lambda (n)
    (= (× (÷ n 2) 2) n)))
```

Now that we have practiced this way of writing functions, *evens-only** is just an exercise:

```
(define evens-only*
  (lambda (l)
    (cond
      ((null? l) (quote ()))
      ((atom? (car l))
       (cond
         ((even? (car l))
          (cons (car l)
            (evens-only* (cdr l))))
         (else (evens-only* (cdr l)))))
      (else (cons (evens-only* (car l))
              (evens-only* (cdr l)))))))
```

What is the value of (*evens-only** *l*)
where
   l is ((9 1 2 8) 3 10 ((9 9) 7 6) 2)

((2 8) 10 (() 6) 2).

What is the sum of the odd numbers in l where l is ((9 1 2 8) 3 10 ((9 9) 7 6) 2)	$9 + 1 + 3 + 9 + 9 + 7 = 38$.

What is the product of the even numbers in l where l is ((9 1 2 8) 3 10 ((9 9) 7 6) 2)	$2 \times 8 \times 10 \times 6 \times 2 = 1920$.

Can you write the function *evens-only*&co* It builds a nested list of even numbers by removing the odd ones from its argument and simultaneously multiplies the even numbers and sums up the odd numbers that occur in its argument.	This is full of stars!

Here is an outline. Can you explain what (*evens-only*&co* (*car l*) ...) accomplishes?

It visits every number in the *car* of l and collects the list without odd numbers, the product of the even numbers, and the sum of the odd numbers.

```
(define evens-only*&co
  (lambda (l col)
    (cond
      ((null? l)
       (col (quote ()) 1 0))
      ((atom? (car l))
       (cond
         ((even? (car l))
          (evens-only*&co (cdr l)
            (lambda (newl p s)
              (col (cons (car l) newl)
                (× (car l) p) s))))
         (else (evens-only*&co (cdr l)
                 (lambda (newl p s)
                   (col newl
                     p (+ (car l) s)))))))
      (else (evens-only*&co (car l)
              ...)))))
```

What does the function *evens-only*&co* do after visiting all the numbers in (*car l*)	It uses the collector, which we haven't defined yet.

And what does the collector do?	It uses *evens-only*&co* to visit the *cdr* of *l* and to collect the list that is like (*cdr l*), without the odd numbers of course, as well as the product of the even numbers and the sum of the odd numbers.

Does this mean the unknown collector looks roughly like this:
 	
    (**lambda** (*al ap as*)
     (*evens-only*&co* (*cdr l*)
      ...))
	Yes.

And when (*evens-only*&co* (*cdr l*) ...) is done with its job, what happens then?	The yet-to-be-determined collector is used, just as before.

What does the collector for
    (*evens-only*&co* (*cdr l*) ...)
do?
	It *cons*es together the results for the lists in the *car* and the *cdr* and multiplies and adds the respective products and sums. Then it passes these values to the old collector:
	
	    (**lambda** (*al ap as*)
	     (*evens-only*&co* (*cdr l*)
	      (**lambda** (*dl dp ds*)
	       (*col* (*cons al dl*)
	        (× *ap dp*)
	        (✢ *as ds*)))))).

Does this all make sense now?	Perfect.

What is the value of
    (*evens-only*&co l the-last-friend*)
where
   l is ((9 1 2 8) 3 10 ((9 9) 7 6) 2) and
   the-last-friend is defined as follows:
 	
  (**define** *the-last-friend*
   (**lambda** (*newl product sum*)
    (*cons sum*
     (*cons product*
      newl))))
	(38 1920 (2 8) 10 (() 6) 2).

Whew! Is your brain twisted up now?   Go eat a pretzel; don't forget the mustard.

9.
...and Again, and Again, and Again,...

Are you in the mood for caviar	Then we must go *looking* for it.

What is (*looking* *a* *lat*)
where *a* is caviar
and
   lat is (6 2 4 caviar 5 7 3)
	#t ,
	   caviar is obviously in *lat*.

(*looking* *a* *lat*) where *a* is caviar and *lat* is (6 2 grits caviar 5 7 3)	#f.
Were you expecting something different?	Yes, caviar is still in *lat*.
True enough, but what is the first number in the lat?	6.
And what is the sixth element of *lat*	7.
And what is the seventh element?	3.

So *looking* clearly can't find caviar	True enough,
	   because the third element is grits, which
	   does not even resemble caviar.

Here is *looking*	We did not expect you to know this.

```
(define looking
  (lambda (a lat)
    (keep-looking a (pick 1 lat) lat)))
```

Write *keep-looking*	

(*looking* *a* *lat*)
where *a* is caviar
and
   lat is (6 2 4 caviar 5 7 3)
	#t ,
	   because (*keep-looking* *a* 6 *lat*) has the same
	   answer as (*keep-looking* *a* (*pick* 1 *lat*) *lat*).

What is (*pick* 6 *lat*) where *lat* is (6 2 4 caviar 5 7 3)	7.

So what do we do?	(*keep-looking* *a* 7 *lat*) where *a* is caviar and *lat* is (6 2 4 caviar 5 7 3).

What is (*pick* 7 *lat*) where *lat* is (6 2 4 caviar 5 7 3)	3.

So what is (*keep-looking* *a* 3 *lat*)
where *a* is caviar
and
  lat is (6 2 4 caviar 5 7 3)
	It is the same as
	  (*keep-looking* *a* 4 *lat*).

Which is?	#t .

Write *keep-looking*	<pre>(**define** *keep-looking*
	  (**lambda** (*a sorn lat*)
	    (**cond**
	      ((*number? sorn*)
	       (*keep-looking a* (*pick sorn lat*) *lat*))
	      (**else** (*eq? sorn a*)))))</pre>

Can you guess what *sorn* stands for?	Symbol or number.

What is unusual about *keep-looking*	It does not recur on a part of *lat*.

We call this "unnatural" recursion.	It is truly unnatural.

Does *keep-looking* appear to get closer to its goal?	Yes, from all available evidence.
Does it always get closer to its goal?	Sometimes the list may contain neither caviar nor grits.
That is correct. A list may be a tup.	Yes, if we start *looking* in (7 2 4 7 5 6 3), we will never stop looking.
What is (*looking a lat*) where *a* is caviar and *lat* is (7 1 2 caviar 5 6 3)	This is strange!
Yes, it is strange. What happens?	We keep looking and looking and looking . . .
Functions like *looking* are called partial functions. What do you think the functions we have seen so far are called?	They are called total.

Can you define a shorter function that does not reach its goal for some of its arguments?	(**define** *eternity*
	  (**lambda** (*x*)
	    (*eternity x*)))

For how many of its arguments does *eternity* reach its goal?	None, and this is the most unnatural recursion possible.
Is *eternity* partial?	It is the most partial function.
What is (*shift x*) where *x* is ((a b) c)	(a (b c)).

What is (*shift x*)
where
  x is ((a b) (c d))

(a (b (c d))).

Define *shift*

This is trivial; it's not even recursive!

> (**define** *shift*
>   (**lambda** (*pair*)
>   (*build* (*first* (*first pair*))
>   (*build* (*second* (*first pair*))
>   (*second pair*)))))

Describe what *shift* does.

Here are our words:
  "The function *shift* takes a pair whose first
  component is a pair and builds a pair by
  shifting the second part of the first
  component into the second component."

Now look at this function:

> (**define** *align*
>   (**lambda** (*pora*)
>   (**cond**
>   ((*atom? pora*) *pora*)
>   ((*a-pair?* (*first pora*))
>   (*align* (*shift pora*)))
>   (**else** (*build* (*first pora*)
>   (*align* (*second pora*)))))))

What does it have in common with
keep-looking

Both functions change their arguments for
their recursive uses but in neither case is the
change guaranteed to get us closer to the
goal.

Why are we not guaranteed that *align* makes
progress?

In the second **cond**-line *shift* creates an
argument for *align* that is not a part of the
original argument.

Which commandment does that violate?

The Seventh Commandment.

Is the new argument at least smaller than the original one?	It does not look that way.
Why not?	The function *shift* only rearranges the pair it gets.
And?	Both the result and the argument of *shift* have the same number of atoms.
Can you write a function that counts the number of atoms in *align*'s arguments?	No problem:

```
(define length*
  (lambda (pora)
    (cond
      ((atom? pora) 1)
      (else
        (+ (length* (first pora))
           (length* (second pora)))))))
```

Is *align* a partial function?	We don't know yet. There may be arguments for which it keeps aligning things.
Is there something else that changes about the arguments to *align* and its recursive uses?	Yes, there is. The first component of a pair becomes simpler, though the second component becomes more complicated.
In what way is the first component simpler?	It is only a part of the original pair's first component.
Doesn't this mean that *length** is the wrong function for determining the length of the argument? Can you find a better function?	A better function should pay more attention to the first component.
How much more attention should we pay to the first component?	At least twice as much.

Do you mean something like *weight**

That looks right.

```
(define weight*
  (lambda (pora)
    (cond
      ((atom? pora) 1)
      (else
        (+ (× (weight* (first pora)) 2)
           (weight* (second pora)))))))
```

What is (*weight** *x*)
where
  x is ((a b) c)

7.

And what is (*weight** *x*)
where
  x is (a (b c))

5.

Does this mean that the arguments get simpler?

Yes, the *weight**'s of *align*'s arguments become successively smaller.

Is *align* a partial function?

No, it yields a value for every argument.

Here is *shuffle* which is like *align* but uses *revpair* from chapter 7, instead of *shift*:

The functions *shuffle* and *revpair* swap the components of pairs when the first component is a pair.

```
(define shuffle
  (lambda (pora)
    (cond
      ((atom? pora) pora)
      ((a-pair? (first pora))
       (shuffle (revpair pora)))
      (else (build (first pora)
                   (shuffle (second pora)))))))
```

Does this mean that *shuffle* is total?

We don't know.

Let's try it. What is the value of (*shuffle x*) where *x* is (a (b c))	(a (b c)).

(*shuffle x*) where *x* is (a b)	(a b).

Okay, let's try something interesting. What is the value of (*shuffle x*) where *x* is ((a b) (c d))	To determine this value, we need to find out what (*shuffle* (*revpair pora*)) is where *pora* is ((a b) (c d)).

And how are we going to do that?	We are going to determine the value of (*shuffle pora*) where *pora* is ((c d) (a b)).

Doesn't this mean that we need to know the value of (*shuffle* (*revpair pora*)) where (*revpair pora*) is ((a b) (c d))	Yes, we do.

And?	The function *shuffle* is not total because it now swaps the components of the pair again, which means that we start all over.

Is this function total?	It doesn't yield a value for 0, but otherwise nobody knows. Thank you, Lothar Collatz (1910–1990).

```
(define C
  (lambda (n)
    (cond
      ((one? n) 1)
      (else
        (cond
          ((even? n) (C (÷ n 2)))
          (else (C (add1 (× 3 n)))))))))
```

What is the value of $(A\ 1\ 0)$	2.

$(A\ 1\ 1)$	3.

$(A\ 2\ 2)$	7.

Here is the definition of A

```
(define A
  (lambda (n m)
    (cond
      ((zero? n) (add1 m))
      ((zero? m) (A (sub1 n) 1))
      (else (A (sub1 n)
               (A n (sub1 m)))))))
```

Thank you, Wilhelm Ackermann (1853–1946).

What does A have in common with *shuffle* and *looking*	A's arguments, like *shuffle*'s and *looking*'s, do not necessarily decrease for the recursion.

How about an example?	That's easy: $(A\ 1\ 2)$ needs the value of $(A\ 0\ (A\ 1\ 1))$. And that means we need the value of $(A\ 0\ 3)$.

Does A always give an answer?	Yes, it is total.

Then what is $(A\ 4\ 3)$	For all practical purposes, there is no answer.

What does that mean?	The page that you are reading now will have decayed long before we could possibly have calculated the value of $(A\ 4\ 3)$.

> But answer came there none—
>   And this was scarcely odd, because
> They'd eaten every one.
>
> The Walrus and The Carpenter
>   —*Lewis Carroll*

Wouldn't it be great if we could write a function that tells us whether some function returns with a value for every argument?	It sure would. Now that we have seen functions that never return a value or return a value so late that it is too late, we should have some tool like this around.
Okay, let's write it.	It sounds complicated. A function can work for many different arguments.
Then let's make it simpler. For a warm-up exercise, let's focus on a function that checks whether some function stops for just the empty list, the simplest of all arguments.	That would simplify it a lot.

Here is the beginning of this function:

```
(define will-stop?
  (lambda (f)
    ...))
```

Can you fill in the dots?

What does it do?

Does *will-stop?* return a value for all arguments?	That's the easy part: we said that it either returns #t or #f, depending on whether the argument stops when applied to ().
Is *will-stop?* total then?	Yes, it is. It always returns #t or #f.
Then let's make up some examples. Here is the first one. What is the value of (*will-stop?* f) where f is *length*	We know that (*length l*) is 0 where *l* is ().
So?	Then the value of (*will-stop? length*) should be #t.

Absolutely. How about another example? What is the value of (*will-stop? eternity*)	(*eternity* (**quote** ())) doesn't return a value. We just saw that.
Does this mean the value of (*will-stop? eternity*) is #f	Yes, it does.
Do we need more examples?	Perhaps we should do one more example.

Okay, here is a function that could be an interesting argument for *will-stop?*
 	
(**define** *last-try*
  (**lambda** (*x*)
    (**and** (*will-stop? last-try*)
     (*eternity x*))))
 	
What is (*will-stop? last-try*)
	What does it do?

We need to test it on ()	If we want the value of (*last-try* (**quote** ())), we must determine the value of
	  (**and** (*will-stop? last-try*)
	    (*eternity* (**quote** ()))).

What is the value of
  (**and** (*will-stop? last-try*)
    (*eternity* (**quote** ())))
	That depends on the value of
	  (*will-stop? last-try*).

There are only two possibilities. Let's say (*will-stop? last-try*) is #f	Okay, then (**and** #f (*eternity* (**quote** ()))), is #f, since (**and** #f ...) is always #f.
So (*last-try* (**quote** ())) stopped, right?	Yes, it did.
But didn't *will-stop?* predict just the opposite?	Yes, it did. We said that the value of (*will-stop? last-try*) was #f, which really means that *last-try* will not stop.

So we must have been wrong about (*will-stop? last-try*)	That's correct. It must return #t, because *will-stop?* always gives an answer. We said it was total.
Fine. If (*will-stop? last-try*) is #t what is the value of (*last-try* (**quote** ()))	Now we just need to determine the value of (**and** #t (*eternity* (**quote** ()))), which is the same as the value of (*eternity* (**quote** ())).
What is the value of (*eternity* (**quote** ()))	It doesn't have a value. We know that it doesn't stop.
But that means we were wrong again!	True, since this time we said that (*will-stop? last-try*) was #t .
What do you think this means?	Here is our meaning: "We took a really close look at the two possible cases. If we can **define** *will-stop?*, then (*will-stop? last-try*) must yield either #t or #f. But it cannot—due to the very definition of what *will-stop?* is supposed to do. This must mean that *will-stop?* cannot be **define**d."
Is this unique?	Yes, it is. It makes *will-stop?* the first function that we can describe precisely but cannot **define** in our language.
Is there any way around this problem?	No. Thank you, Alan M. Turing (1912–1954) and Kurt Gödel (1906–1978).
What is (**define** ...)	This is an interesting question. We just saw that (**define** ...) doesn't work for *will-stop?*.

So what are recursive definitions?	Hold tight, take a deep breath, and plunge forward when you're ready.

Is this the function *length*

```
(define length
  (lambda (l)
    (cond
      ((null? l) 0)
      (else (add1 (length (cdr l)))))))
```

It sure is.

What if we didn't have (**define** ...) anymore? Could we still define *length*

Without (**define** ...) nothing, and especially not the body of *length*, could refer to *length*.

What does this function do?

```
(lambda (l)
  (cond
    ((null? l) 0)
    (else (add1 (eternity (cdr l))))))
```

It determines the length of the empty list and nothing else.

What happens when we use it on a non-empty list?

No answer. If we give *eternity* an argument, it gives no answer.

What does it mean for this function that looks like *length*

It just won't give any answer for non-empty lists.

Suppose we could name this new function. What would be a good name?

$length_0$
  because the function can only determine the length of the empty list.

How would you write a function that determines the length of lists that contain one or fewer items?

Well, we could try the following.

```
(lambda (l)
  (cond
    ((null? l) 0)
    (else (add1 (length₀ (cdr l))))))
```

Almost, but (**define** ...) doesn't work for $length_0$

So, replace $length_0$ by its definition.

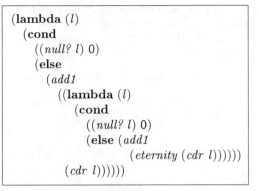

And what's a good name for this function?

That's easy: $length_{\leq 1}$.

Is this the function that would determine the lenghts of lists that contain two or fewer items?

Yes, this is $length_{\leq 2}$. We just replace *eternity* with the next version of *length*.

```
(lambda (l)
  (cond
    ((null? l) 0)
    (else
      (add1
        ((lambda (l)
          (cond
            ((null? l) 0)
            (else
              (add1
                ((lambda (l)
                  (cond
                    ((null? l) 0)
                    (else
                      (add1
                        (eternity
                          (cdr l))))))
                  (cdr l))))))
          (cdr l))))))
```

Now, what do you think recursion is?

What do you mean?

Well, we have seen how to determine the length of a list with no items, with no more than one item, with no more than two items, and so on. How could we get the function *length* back?

If we could write an infinite function in the style of $length_0$, $length_{\leq 1}$, $length_{\leq 2}$, ..., then we could write $length_\infty$, which would determine the length of all lists that we can make.

How long are the lists that we can make?

Well, a list is either empty, or it contains one element, or two elements, or three, or four, ..., or 1001, ...

But we can't write an infinite function.

No, we can't.

And we still have all these repetitions and patterns in these functions.

Yes, we do.

What do these patterns look like?

All these programs contain a function that looks like *length*. Perhaps we should abstract out this function: see The Ninth Commandment.

Let's do it!

We need a function that looks just like *length* but starts with (**lambda** (*length*) ...).

Do you mean this?

Yes, that's okay. It creates $length_0$.

```
((lambda (length)
   (lambda (l)
     (cond
       ((null? l) 0)
       (else (add1 (length (cdr l)))))))
 eternity)
```

Rewrite $length_{\leq 1}$ in the same style.

```
((lambda (f)
   (lambda (l)
     (cond
       ((null? l) 0)
       (else (add1 (f (cdr l)))))))
 ((lambda (g)
    (lambda (l)
      (cond
        ((null? l) 0)
        (else (add1 (g (cdr l)))))))
  eternity))
```

Do we have to use *length* to name the argument?

No, we just used *f* and *g*. As long as we are consistent, everything's okay.

How about $length_{\leq 2}$

```
((lambda (length)
   (lambda (l)
     (cond
       ((null? l) 0)
       (else (add1 (length (cdr l)))))))
 ((lambda (length)
    (lambda (l)
      (cond
        ((null? l) 0)
        (else (add1 (length (cdr l)))))))
  ((lambda (length)
     (lambda (l)
       (cond
         ((null? l) 0)
         (else (add1 (length (cdr l)))))))
   eternity)))
```

Close, but there are still repetitions.

True. Let's get rid of them.

Where should we start?

Name the function that takes *length* as an argument and that returns a function that looks like *length*.

... and Again, and Again, and Again, ...

What's a good name for this function?	How about *mk-length* for "make *length*"?

Okay, do this to $length_0$

No problem.

```
((lambda (mk-length)
   (mk-length eternity))
 (lambda (length)
   (lambda (l)
     (cond
       ((null? l) 0)
       (else (add1 (length (cdr l)))))))))
```

Is this $length_{\leq 1}$

It sure is. And this is $length_{\leq 2}$.

```
((lambda (mk-length)
   (mk-length
     (mk-length eternity)))
 (lambda (length)
   (lambda (l)
     (cond
       ((null? l) 0)
       (else (add1 (length (cdr l))))))))
```

```
((lambda (mk-length)
   (mk-length
     (mk-length
       (mk-length eternity))))
 (lambda (length)
   (lambda (l)
     (cond
       ((null? l) 0)
       (else (add1 (length (cdr l))))))))
```

Can you write $length_{\leq 3}$ in this style?

Sure. Here it is.

```
((lambda (mk-length)
   (mk-length
     (mk-length
       (mk-length
         (mk-length eternity)))))
 (lambda (length)
   (lambda (l)
     (cond
       ((null? l) 0)
       (else (add1 (length (cdr l))))))))
```

What is recursion like?

It is like an infinite tower of applications of *mk-length* to an arbitrary function.

Do we really need an infinite tower?	Not really of course. Everytime we use *length* we only need a finite number, but we never know how many.
Could we guess how many we need?	Sure, but we may not guess a large enough number.
When do we find out that we didn't guess a large enough number?	When we apply the function *eternity* that is passed to the innermost *mk-length*.
What if we could create another application of *mk-length* to *eternity* at this point?	That would only postpone the problem by one, and besides, how could we do that?
Well, since nobody cares what function we pass to *mk-length* we could pass it *mk-length* initially.	That's the right idea. And then we invoke *mk-length* on *eternity* and the result of this on the *cdr* so that we get one more piece of the tower.

Then is this still *length*$_0$

```
((lambda (mk-length)
   (mk-length mk-length))
 (lambda (length)
   (lambda (l)
     (cond
       ((null? l) 0)
       (else (add1
               (length (cdr l))))))))
```

Yes, we could even use *mk-length* instead of *length*.

```
((lambda (mk-length)
   (mk-length mk-length))
 (lambda (mk-length)
   (lambda (l)
     (cond
       ((null? l) 0)
       (else (add1
               (mk-length (cdr l))))))))
```

Why would we want to do that?	All names are equal, but some names are more equal than others.[1]

---

[1] With apologies to George Orwell (1903-1950).

True: as long as we use the names consistently, we are just fine.

And *mk-length* is a far more equal name than *length*. If we use a name like *mk-length*, it is a constant reminder that the first argument to *mk-length* is *mk-length*.

Now that *mk-length* is passed to *mk-length* can we use the argument to create an additional recursive use?

Yes, when we apply *mk-length* once, we get $length_{\leq 1}$

```
((lambda (mk-length)
   (mk-length mk-length))
 (lambda (mk-length)
   (lambda (l)
     (cond
       ((null? l) 0)
       (else (add1
               ((mk-length eternity)
                (cdr l)))))))))
```

What is the value of

```
(((lambda (mk-length)
    (mk-length mk-length))
  (lambda (mk-length)
    (lambda (l)
      (cond
        ((null? l) 0)
        (else (add1
                ((mk-length eternity)
                 (cdr l))))))))
  l)
```

where
  l is (apples)

This is a good exercise. Work it out with paper and pencil.

Could we do this more than once?

Yes, just keep passing *mk-length* to itself, and we can do this as often as we need to!

What would you call this function?

```
((lambda (mk-length)
   (mk-length mk-length))
 (lambda (mk-length)
   (lambda (l)
     (cond
       ((null? l) 0)
       (else (add1
               ((mk-length mk-length)
                (cdr l)))))))))
```

It is *length*, of course.

How does it work?

It keeps adding recursive uses by passing *mk-length* to itself, just as it is about to expire.

One problem is left: it no longer contains the function that looks like *length*

```
((lambda (mk-length)
   (mk-length mk-length))
 (lambda (mk-length)
   (lambda (l)
     (cond
       ((null? l) 0)
       (else (add1
               ((mk-length mk-length)
                (cdr l)))))))))
```

Can you fix that?

We could extract this new application of *mk-length* to itself and call it *length*.

Why?

Because it really makes the function *length*.

How about this?

```
((lambda (mk-length)
   (mk-length mk-length))
 (lambda (mk-length)
   ((lambda (length)
      (lambda (l)
        (cond
          ((null? l) 0)
          (else (add1 (length (cdr l)))))))
    (mk-length mk-length))))
```

Yes, this looks just fine.

Let's see whether it works.

Okay.

What is the value of

```
(((lambda (mk-length)
    (mk-length mk-length))
  (lambda (mk-length)
    ((lambda (length)
       (lambda (l)
         (cond
           ((null? l) 0)
           (else (add1 (length (cdr l)))))))
     (mk-length mk-length))))
 l)
```

where
  l is (apples)

It should be 1.

First, we need the value of

```
((lambda (mk-length)
   (mk-length mk-length))
 (lambda (mk-length)
   ((lambda (length)
      (lambda (l)
        (cond
          ((null? l) 0)
          (else (add1 (length (cdr l)))))))
    (mk-length mk-length))))
```

That's true, because the value of this expression is the function that we need to apply to *l* where
  l is (apples)

So we really need the value of
```
((lambda (mk-length)
   ((lambda (length)
      (lambda (l)
        (cond
          ((null? l) 0)
          (else (add1 (length (cdr l)))))))
    (mk-length mk-length)))
 (lambda (mk-length)
   ((lambda (length)
      (lambda (l)
        (cond
          ((null? l) 0)
          (else (add1 (length (cdr l)))))))
    (mk-length mk-length))))
```

True enough.

But then we really need to know the value of
```
((lambda (length)
   (lambda (l)
     (cond
       ((null? l) 0)
       (else (add1 (length (cdr l)))))))
 ((lambda (mk-length)
    ((lambda (length)
       (lambda (l)
         (cond
           ((null? l) 0)
           (else (add1 (length (cdr l)))))))
     (mk-length mk-length)))
  (lambda (mk-length)
    ((lambda (length)
       (lambda (l)
         (cond
           ((null? l) 0)
           (else (add1 (length (cdr l)))))))
     (mk-length mk-length)))))
```

Yes, that's true, too. Where is the end of this? Don't we also need to know the value of
```
((lambda (length)
   (lambda (l)
     (cond
       ((null? l) 0)
       (else (add1 (length (cdr l)))))))
 ((lambda (length)
    (lambda (l)
      (cond
        ((null? l) 0)
        (else (add1 (length (cdr l)))))))
  ((lambda (mk-length)
     ((lambda (length)
        (lambda (l)
          (cond
            ((null? l) 0)
            (else (add1 (length (cdr l)))))))
      (mk-length mk-length)))
   (lambda (mk-length)
     ((lambda (length)
        (lambda (l)
          (cond
            ((null? l) 0)
            (else (add1 (length (cdr l)))))))
      (mk-length mk-length))))))
```

Yes, there is no end to it. Why?	Because we just keep applying *mk-length* to itself again and again and again ...

Is this strange?	It is because *mk-length* used to return a function when we applied it to an argument. Indeed, it didn't matter what we applied it to.

But now that we have extracted (*mk-length mk-length*) from the function that makes *length* it does not return a function anymore.	No it doesn't. So what do we do?

Turn the application of *mk-length* to itself in our last correct version of *length* into a function:

```
((lambda (mk-length)
   (mk-length mk-length))
 (lambda (mk-length)
   (lambda (l)
     (cond
       ((null? l) 0)
       (else (add1
               ((mk-length mk-length)
                (cdr l)))))))))
```

How?

Here is a different way. If *f* is a function of one argument, is (**lambda** (*x*) (*f x*)) a function of one argument?	Yes, it is.

If (*mk-length mk-length*) returns a function of one argument, does
    (**lambda** (*x*)
      ((*mk-length mk-length*) *x*))
return a function of one argument?
	Actually,
	    (**lambda** (*x*)
	      ((*mk-length mk-length*) *x*))
	is a function!

Okay, let's do this to the application of *mk-length* to itself.

```
((lambda (mk-length)
   (mk-length mk-length))
 (lambda (mk-length)
   (lambda (l)
     (cond
       ((null? l) 0)
       (else
         (add1
           ((lambda (x)
              ((mk-length mk-length) x))
            (cdr l)))))))))
```

Move out the new function so that we get *length* back.

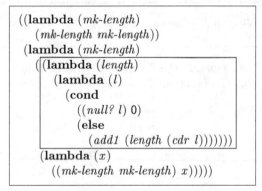

```
((lambda (mk-length)
   (mk-length mk-length))
 (lambda (mk-length)
   ((lambda (length)
      (lambda (l)
        (cond
          ((null? l) 0)
          (else
            (add1 (length (cdr l)))))))
    (lambda (x)
      ((mk-length mk-length) x)))))
```

Is it okay to move out the function?

Yes, we just always did the opposite by replacing a name with its value. Here we extract a value and give it a name.

Can we extract the function in the box that looks like *length* and give it a name?

Yes, it does not depend on *mk-length* at all!

Is this the right function?

Yes.

```
((lambda (le)
   ((lambda (mk-length)
      (mk-length mk-length))
    (lambda (mk-length)
      (le (lambda (x)
            ((mk-length mk-length) x))))))
 (lambda (length)
   (lambda (l)
     (cond
       ((null? l) 0)
       (else (add1 (length (cdr l)))))))))
```

What did we actually get back?

We extracted the original function *mk-length*.

Let's separate the function that makes *length* from the function that looks like *length*

That's easy.

```
(lambda (le)
  ((lambda (mk-length)
     (mk-length mk-length))
   (lambda (mk-length)
     (le (lambda (x)
           ((mk-length mk-length) x))))))
```

Does this function have a name?

Yes, it is called the applicative-order Y combinator.

```
(define Y
  (lambda (le)
    ((lambda (f) (f f))
     (lambda (f)
       (le (lambda (x) ((f f) x)))))))
```

Does (**define** ...) work again?

Sure, now that we know what recursion is.

Do you now know why Y works?

Read this chapter just one more time and you will.

What is $(Y\ Y)$	Who knows, but it works very hard.

Does your hat still fit?	Perhaps not after such a mind stretcher.

Stop the World—I Want to Get Off.
Leslie Bricusse and Anthony Newley

10.
What Is the Value of All of This?

An entry is a pair of lists whose first list is a set. Also, the two lists must be of equal length. Make up some examples for entries.	Here are our examples:
	
	  ((appetizer entrée beverage)
	   (paté boeuf vin))
	and
	  ((appetizer entrée beverage)
	   (beer beer beer))
	and
	  ((beverage dessert)
	   ((food is) (number one with us))).

How can we build an entry from a set of names and a list of values?	(**define** *new-entry build*) Try to build our examples with this function.

What is (*lookup-in-entry name entry*)
where *name* is entrée
and
   entry is ((appetizer entrée beverage)
        (food tastes good))
	tastes.

What if *name* is dessert	In this case we would like to leave the decision about what to do with the user of *lookup-in-entry*.
How can we accomplish this?	*lookup-in-entry* takes an additional argument that is invoked when *name* is not found in the first list of an entry.
How many arguments do you think this extra function should take?	We think it should take one, *name*. Why?

Here is our definition of *lookup-in-entry*

```
(define lookup-in-entry
  (lambda (name entry entry-f)
    (lookup-in-entry-help name
      (first entry)
      (second entry)
      entry-f)))
```

Finish the function *lookup-in-entry-help*

```
(define lookup-in-entry-help
  (lambda (name names values entry-f)
    (cond
      ( _____ _____ )
      ( _____ _____ )
      ( _____ _____ ))))
```

```
(define lookup-in-entry-help
  (lambda (name names values entry-f)
    (cond
      ((null? names) (entry-f name))
      ((eq? (car names) name)
       (car values))
      (else (lookup-in-entry-help name
              (cdr names)
              (cdr values)
              entry-f)))))
```

A table (also called an environment) is a list of entries. Here is one example: the empty table, represented by ()
Make up some others.

Here is another one:
(((appetizer entrée beverage)
  (paté boeuf vin))
 ((beverage dessert)
  ((food is) (number one with us)))).

Define the function *extend-table* which takes an entry and a table (possibly the empty one) and creates a new table by putting the new entry in front of the old table.

```
(define extend-table cons)
```

What is
  (lookup-in-table name table table-f)
where
  name is entrée
  table is (((entrée dessert)
            (spaghetti spumoni))
           ((appetizer entrée beverage)
            (food tastes good)))
and
  table-f is (lambda (name) ...)

It could be either spaghetti or tastes, but *lookup-in-table* searches the list of entries in order. So it is spaghetti.

Write *lookup-in-table*
    Hint: Don't forget to get some help.
	```(define lookup-in-table```
	 ``` (lambda (name table table-f)```
	 ``` (cond```
	 ``` ((null? table) (table-f name))```
	 ``` (else (lookup-in-entry name```
	 ``` (car table)```
	 ``` (lambda (name)```
	 ``` (lookup-in-table name```
	 ``` (cdr table)```
	 ``` table-f)))))))```

Can you describe what the following function represents:

```
(lambda (name)
  (lookup-in-table name
    (cdr table)
    table-f))
```

This function is the action to take when the name is not found in the first entry.

In the preface we mentioned that sans serif typeface would be used to represent atoms. To this point it has not mattered. Henceforth, you must notice whether or not an atom is in sans serif.

Remember to be very conscious as to whether or not an atom is in sans serif.

Did you notice that "sans serif" was not in sans serif?

We hope so. This is "sans serif"
                    in sans serif.

Have we chosen a good representation for expressions?

Yes. They are all S-expressions so they can be data for functions.

What kind of functions?

For example, *value*.

Do you remember *value* from chapter 6?

Recall that *value* is the function that returns the natural value of expressions.

What is the value of

```
(car (quote (a b c)))
```

We don't even know what (**quote** (a b c)) is.

What is the value of
  (*cons rep-a*
    (*cons rep-b*
      (*cons rep-c*
        (**quote** ())))))
where
  rep-a is a
  rep-b is b
and
  rep-c is c
	It is the same as (a b c).

Great. And what is the value of
  (*cons rep-car*
    (*cons* (*cons rep-quote*
          (*cons*
            (*cons rep-a*
             (*cons rep-b*
              (*cons rep-c*
                (**quote** ())))))
          (**quote** ()))))
      (**quote** ()))))
where
  rep-car is car
  rep-quote is quote
  rep-a is a
  rep-b is b
and
  rep-c is c
	It is a representation of the expression:
	  (car (quote (a b c))).

What is the value of (*car* (**quote** (a b c)))	a.

What is (*value e*) where *e* is (car (quote (a b c)))	a.

What is (*value e*) where *e* is (quote (car (quote (a b c))))	(car (quote (a b c))).

What is (*value e*) where *e* is (add1 6)	7.
What is (*value e*) where *e* is 6	6, because numbers are constants.
What is (*value e*) where *e* is (quote nothing)	nothing.
What is (*value e*) where *e* is nothing	nothing has no value.

What is (*value e*)
where
  e is ((lambda (nothing)
      (cons nothing (quote ()))))
   (quote
    (from nothing comes something)))
	((from nothing comes something)).

What is (*value e*)
where
  e is ((lambda (nothing)
    (cond
      (nothing (quote something))
      (else (quote nothing))))
   #t)
	something.

What is the type of *e* where *e* is 6	*const*.
What is the type of *e* where *e* is #f	*const*.

What is (*value e*) where *e* is #f	#f.
What is the type of *e* where *e* is cons	*const.*
What is (*value e*) where *e* is car	(primitive car).
What is the type of *e* where *e* is (quote nothing)	*quote.*
What is the type of *e* where *e* is nothing	*identifier.*
What is the type of *e* where *e* is (lambda (x y) (cons x y))	*lambda.*

What is the type of *e*
where
  e is ((lambda (nothing)
      (cond
        (nothing (quote something))
        (else (quote nothing))))
    #t)

application.

What is the type of *e*
where
  e is (cond
      (nothing (quote something))
      (else (quote nothing)))

cond.

How many types do you think there are?

We found six:
const
quote
identifier
lambda
cond
and
application.

How do you think we should represent types?

We choose functions. We call these functions "actions."

If actions are functions that do "the right thing" when applied to the appropriate type of expression, what should *value* do?

You guessed it. It would have to find out the type of expression it was passed and then use the associated action,

Do you remember *atom-to-function* from chapter 8?

We found *atom-to-function* useful when we rewrote *value* for numbered expresssions.

Below is a function that produces the correct action (or function) for each possible S-expression:

```
(define expression-to-action
  (lambda (e)
    (cond
      ((atom? e) (atom-to-action e))
      (else (list-to-action e)))))
```

Define the function *atom-to-action*[1]

```
(define atom-to-action
  (lambda (e)
    (cond
      ((number? e) *const)
      ((eq? e #t) *const)
      ((eq? e #f) *const)
      ((eq? e (quote cons)) *const)
      ((eq? e (quote car)) *const)
      ((eq? e (quote cdr)) *const)
      ((eq? e (quote null?)) *const)
      ((eq? e (quote eq?)) *const)
      ((eq? e (quote atom?)) *const)
      ((eq? e (quote zero?)) *const)
      ((eq? e (quote add1)) *const)
      ((eq? e (quote sub1)) *const)
      ((eq? e (quote number?)) *const)
      (else *identifier))))
```

[1] Ill-formed S-expressions such as (quote a b), (), (lambda (#t) #t), (lambda (5) 5), (lambda (car) car), (lambda a), (cond (3 c) (else b) (6 a)), and (1 2) are not considered here. They can be detected by an appropriate function to which S-expressions are submitted before they are passed on to *value*.

Now define the help function *list-to-action*

```
(define list-to-action
  (lambda (e)
    (cond
      ((atom? (car e))
       (cond
         ((eq? (car e) (quote quote))
          *quote)
         ((eq? (car e) (quote lambda))
          *lambda)
         ((eq? (car e) (quote cond))
          *cond)
         (else *application)))
      (else *application))))
```

Assuming that *expression-to-action* works, we can use it to define *value* and *meaning*

```
(define value
  (lambda (e)
    (meaning e (quote ()))))
```

```
(define meaning
  (lambda (e table)
    ((expression-to-action e) e table)))
```

What is (quote ()) in the definition of *value*

It is the empty table. The function *value*,[1] together with all the functions it uses, is called an interpreter.

---

[1] The function *value* approximates the function **eval** available in Scheme (and Lisp).

Actions do speak louder than words.

How many arguments should actions take according to the above?

Two, the expression *e* and a table.

Here is the action for constants.

```
(define *const
  (lambda (e table)
    (cond
      ((number? e) e)
      ((eq? e #t) #t)
      ((eq? e #f) #f)
      (else (build (quote primitive) e)))))
```

Is it correct?

Yes, for numbers, it just returns the expression, and this is all we have to do for
0, 1, 2, ...
For #t, it returns true.
For #f, it returns false.
And all other atoms of constant type represent primitives.

Here is the action for *quote

```
(define *quote
  (lambda (e table)
    (text-of e)))
```

Define the help function text-of

```
(define text-of second)
```

Have we used the table yet?

No, but we will in a moment.

Why do we need the table?

To remember the values of identifiers.

Given that the table contains the values of identifiers, write the action *identifier

```
(define *identifier
  (lambda (e table)
    (lookup-in-table e table initial-table)))
```

Here is initial-table

```
(define initial-table
  (lambda (name)
    (car (quote ()))))
```

When is it used?

Let's hope never. Why?

What is the value of (lambda (x) x)

We don't know yet, but we know that it must be the representation of a non-primitive function.

What Is the Value of All of This?

How are non-primitive functions different from primitives?	We know what primitives do; non-primitives are defined by their arguments and their function bodies.
So when we want to use a non-primitive we need to remember its formal arguments and its function body.	At least. Fortunately this is just the *cdr* of a lambda expression.
And what else do we need to remember?	We will also put the table in, just in case we might need it later.
And how do we represent this?	In a list, of course.

Here is the action **lambda*

```
(define *lambda
  (lambda (e table)
    (build (quote non-primitive)
      (cons table (cdr e)))))
```

What is (*meaning e table*)
where
  e is (lambda (x) (cons x y))
and
  table is (((y z) ((8) 9)))

(non-primitive
  ((((y z) ((8) 9)))   (x)   (cons x y)))
       table   formals   body

It is probably a good idea to define some help functions for getting back the parts in this three element list (i.e., the table, the formal arguments, and the body). Write *table-of formals-of* and *body-of*	(define *table-of first*)
	(define *formals-of second*)
	(define *body-of third*)
Describe (**cond** ...) in your own words.	It is a special form that takes any number of **cond**-lines. It considers each line in turn. If the question part on the left is false, it looks at the rest of the lines. Otherwise it proceeds to answer the right part. If it sees an **else**-line, it treats that **cond**-line as if its question part were true.

Here is the function *evcon* that does what we just said in words:

```
(define evcon
  (lambda (lines table)
    (cond
      ((else? (question-of (car lines)))
       (meaning (answer-of (car lines))
         table))
      ((meaning (question-of (car lines))
         table)
       (meaning (answer-of (car lines))
         table))
      (else (evcon (cdr lines) table)))))
```

Write *else?* and the help functions *question-of* and *answer-of*

```
(define else?
  (lambda (x)
    (cond
      ((atom? x) (eq? x (quote else)))
      (else #f))))
```

```
(define question-of first)
```

```
(define answer-of second)
```

Didn't we violate The First Commandment?

Yes, we don't ask (*null? lines*), so one of the questions in every **cond** better be true.

Now use the function *evcon* to write the **cond* action.

```
(define *cond
  (lambda (e table)
    (evcon (cond-lines-of e) table)))
```

```
(define cond-lines-of cdr)
```

Aren't these help functions useful?

Yes, they make things quite a bit more readable. But you already knew that.

Do you understand **cond* now?

Perhaps not.

How can you become familiar with it?

The best way is to try an example. A good one is:
  (**cond e table*)
where
  e is (cond (coffee klatsch) (else party))
and
  table is (((coffee) (#t))
              ((klatsch party) (5 (6)))).

What Is the Value of All of This?

Have we seen how the table gets used?	Yes, *lambda* and *identifier* use it.

But how do the identifiers get into the table?	In the only action we have not defined: *application*.

How is an application represented?	An application is a list of expressions whose *car* position contains an expression whose value is a function.

How does an application differ from a special form, like (**and** ...) (**or** ...) or (**cond** ...)	An application must always determine the meaning of all its arguments.

Before we can apply a function, do we have to get the meaning of all of its arguments?	Yes.

Write a function *evlis* that takes a list of (representations of) arguments and a table, and returns a list composed of the meaning of each argument.

```
(define evlis
  (lambda (args table)
    (cond
      ((null? args) (quote ()))
      (else
        (cons (meaning (car args) table)
          (evlis (cdr args) table))))))
```

What else do we need before we can determine the meaning of an application?	We need to find out what its *function-of* means.

And what then?	Then we apply the meaning of the function to the meaning of the arguments.

Here is *application*

```
(define *application
  (lambda (e table)
    (apply
      (meaning (function-of e) table)
      (evlis (arguments-of e) table))))
```

Is it correct?

Of course. We just have to define *apply*, *function-of*, and *arguments-of* correctly.

Write *function-of* and *arguments-of*

> (**define** *function-of car*)

> (**define** *arguments-of cdr*)

How many different kinds of functions are there?

Two: primitives and non-primitives.

What are the two representations of functions?

(primitive *primitive-name*) and
(non-primitive (*table formals body*))
    The list (*table formals body*) is called a closure record.

Write *primitive?* and *non-primitive?*

> (**define** *primitive?*
>   (**lambda** (*l*)
>   (*eq?* (*first l*) (**quote** primitive))))

> (**define** *non-primitive?*
>   (**lambda** (*l*)
>   (*eq?* (*first l*) (**quote** non-primitive))))

Now we can write the function *apply*

Here it is:

> (**define** *apply*[1]
>   (**lambda** (*fun vals*)
>   (**cond**
>   ((*primitive? fun*)
>   (*apply-primitive*
>   (*second fun*) *vals*))
>   ((*non-primitive? fun*)
>   (*apply-closure*
>   (*second fun*) *vals*)))))

---

[1] If *fun* does not evaluate to either a primitive or a non-primitive as in the expression ((lambda (x) (x 5)) 3), there is no answer. The function *apply* approximates the function **apply** available in Scheme (and Lisp).

This is the definition of *apply-primitive*

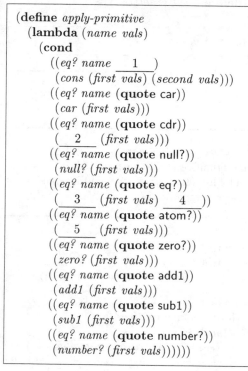

1. (**quote** cons)
2. *cdr*[1]
3. *eq?*
4. (*second vals*)
5. *:atom?*

```
(define :atom?
  (lambda (x)
    (cond
      ((atom? x) #t )
      ((null? x) #f )
      ((eq? (car x) (quote primitive))
       #t )
      ((eq? (car x) (quote non-primitive))
       #t )
      (else #f ))))
```

Fill in the blanks.

---

[1] The function *apply-primitive* could check for applications of *cdr* to the empty list or *sub1* to 0, etc.

Is *apply-closure* the only function left?	Yes, and *apply-closure* must extend the table.

How could we find the result of (f a b) where
  f is (lambda (x y) (cons x y))
  a is 1
and
  b is (2)

That's tricky. But we know what to do to find the meaning of
  (cons x y)
where
  table is (((x y)
              (1 (2)))).

Why can we do this?

Here, we don't need *apply-closure*.

Can you generalize the last two steps?

Applying a non-primitive function—a closure—to a list of values is the same as finding the meaning of the closure's body with its table extended by an entry of the form
(*formals values*)
In this entry, *formals* is the *formals* of the closure and *values* is the result of *evlis*.

Have you followed all this?

If not, here is the definition of *apply-closure*.

```
(define apply-closure
  (lambda (closure vals)
    (meaning (body-of closure)
      (extend-table
        (new-entry
          (formals-of closure)
          vals)
        (table-of closure)))))
```

This is a complicated function and it deserves an example.

In the following,
   closure is ((((u v w)
                   (1 2 3))
                  ((x y z)
                   (4 5 6)))
                 (x y)
                 (cons z x))
and
   vals is ((a b c) (d e f)).

What will be the new arguments of *meaning*

The new *e* for *meaning* will be (cons z x) and the new *table* for *meaning* will be
   (((x y)
     ((a b c) (d e f)))
    ((u v w)
     (1 2 3))
    ((x y z)
     (4 5 6))).

What is the meaning of (*cons z x*)
where *z* is 6
and
  x is (a b c)

The same as
  (*meaning e table*)
where
  e is (cons z x)
and
  table is (((x y)
          ((a b c) (d e f)))
        ((u v w)
        (1 2 3))
        ((x y z)
        (4 5 6))).

Let's find the meaning of all the arguments.
What is
  (*evlis args table*)
where
  args is (z x)
and
  table is (((x y)
          ((a b c) (d e f)))
        ((u v w)
        (1 2 3))
        ((x y z)
        (4 5 6)))

In order to do this, we must find both
  (*meaning e table*)
where
  e is z
and
  (*meaning e table*)
where
  e is x.

What is the (*meaning e table*)
where *e* is z

6, by using **identifier*.

What is (*meaning e table*)
where *e* is x

(a b c), by using **identifier*.

So, what is the result of *evlis*

(6 (a b c)), because *evlis* returns a list of the meanings.

What is (*meaning e table*)
where *e* is cons

(primitive cons), by using **const*.

We are now ready to (*apply fun vals*)
where
    fun is (primitive cons)
and
    vals is (6 (a b c))
Which path should we take?

The *apply-primitive* path.

Which **cond**-line is chosen for
    (*apply-primitive name vals*)
where
    name is cons
and
    vals is (6 (a b c))

The third:
    ((*eq? name* (**quote** cons))
     (*cons* (*first vals*) (*second vals*))).

Are we finished now?

Yes, we are exhausted.

But what about (**define** ...)

It isn't needed because recursion can be obtained from the Y combinator.

Is (**define** ...) really not needed?

Yes, but see *The Seasoned Schemer*.

Does that mean we can run the interpreter on the interpreter if we do the transformation with the Y combinator?

Yes, but don't bother.

What makes *value* unusual?

It sees representations of expressions.

Should *will-stop?* see representations of expressions?

That may help a lot.

Does it help?

No, don't bother—we can play the same game again. We would be able to define a function like *last-try?* that will show that we cannot **define** the new and improved *will-stop?*.

---

else

Yes, it's time for a banquet.

Intermission

You've reached the intermission. What are your options? You could quickly run out and get the rest of the show, *The Seasoned Schemer,* or you could read some of the books that we mention below. All of these books are classics and some of them are quite old; nevertheless they have stood the test of time and are all worthy of your notice. Some have nothing whatsoever to do with mathematics or logic, some have to do with mathematics, but only by way of telling an interesting story, and still others are just worth discovering. There should be no confusion: these books are not here to prepare you to read the sequel, they are just for your entertainment. At the end of *The Seasoned Schemer* you can find a set of references to Scheme and *the* reference to Common Lisp. Do not feel obliged to jump ahead to the next book. Take some time off and read some of these books instead. Then, when you have relaxed a bit, perhaps removed some of the calories that were foisted upon you, go ahead and dive into the sequel. Enjoy!

Abbott, Edwin A. *Flatland.* Dover Publications, Inc., New York, 1952. (Original publication: Seeley and Co., Ltd., London, 1884.)

Carroll, Lewis. *The Annotated Alice: Alice's Adventures in Wonderland and Through the Looking Glass.* Clarkson M. Potter, Inc., New York, 1960. Introduction and notes by Martin Gardner. Original publications under different titles: *Alice's Adventures Under Ground* and *Through the Looking Glass and What Alice Found There*, Macmillan and Company, London 1865 and 1872, respectively.

Halmos, Paul R. *Naive Set Theory.* Litton Educational Publishers, New York, 1960.

Hein, Piet. *Grooks.* The MIT Press, Cambridge, Massachusetts, 1960.

Hofstadter, Douglas R. *Gödel, Escher, Bach: an Eternal Golden Braid.* Basic Books, Inc., New York, 1979.

Nagel, Ernest and James R. Newman. *Gödel's Proof.* New York University Press, New York, 1958.

Pólya, György. *How to Solve It.* Doubleday and Co., New York, 1957.

Smullyan, Raymond. *To Mock a Mockingbird And Other Logic Puzzles Including an Amazing Adventure in Combinatory Logic.* Alfred A. Knopf, Inc., New York, 1985.

Suppes, Patrick. *Introduction to Logic.* Van Nostrand Co., Princeton, New Jersey, 1957.

Index

Index